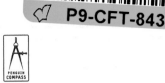

PENGUIN
COMPASS

Many Ways to Nirvana

TENZIN GYATSO, His Holiness the Fourteenth
Dalai Lama, is the spiritual and temporal leader of
the Tibetan people. He was born July 6, 1935, and at
the age of two was recognized as the reincarnation of
the thirteenth Dalai Lama. At the age of fifteen, he
was called upon to assume full responsibility as Head
of State and Government. Following the suppression
of the Tibetan national uprising on March 10, 1959,
His Holiness escaped to India where he was given
political asylum. He is recognized as an advocate of
world peace and interreligious understanding, and he
has received many international awards including the
Nobel Peace Prize in 1989. He travels to the United
States and around the world to lecture and teach.

RENUKA SINGH has a doctorate in sociology from
Jawaharlal Nehru University, New Delhi, where she
is currently an associate professor at the Centre for
the Study of Social Systems. She is also the director
of Tushita Mahayana Meditation Centre, New Delhi.
Additionally, Singh is the editor of two previous
Penguin Compass titles by her spiritual teacher His
Holiness the Dalai Lama, *Live in a Better Way* and
The Path to Tranquility.

Many Ways
to Nirvana

REFLECTIONS
AND ADVICE
ON RIGHT LIVING

His Holiness the Dalai Lama

Edited by Renuka Singh

PENGUIN COMPASS

PENGUIN COMPASS
Published by the Penguin Group
Penguin Group (USA) Inc., 375 Hudson Street,
New York, New York 10014, U.S.A.
Penguin Group (Canada), 90 Eglinton Avenue East, Suite 700,
Toronto, Ontario, Canada M4P 2Y3
(a division of Pearson Penguin Canada Inc.)
Penguin Books Ltd, 80 Strand, London WC2R 0RL, England
Penguin Ireland, 25 St Stephen's Green, Dublin 2, Ireland
(a division of Penguin Books Ltd)
Penguin Group (Australia), 250 Camberwell Road, Camberwell,
Victoria 3124, Australia (a division of Pearson Australia Group Pty Ltd)
Penguin Books India Pvt Ltd, 11 Community Centre,
Panchsheel Park, New Delhi – 110 017, India
Penguin Group (NZ), cnr Airborne and Rosedale Roads,
Albany, Auckland 1310, New Zealand
(a division of Pearson New Zealand Ltd)
Penguin Books (South Africa) (Pty) Ltd, 24 Sturdee Avenue,
Rosebank, Johannesburg 2196, South Africa

Penguin Books Ltd, Registered Offices:
80 Strand, London WC2R 0RL, England

First published in India by Penguin Books India 2004
Published in Penguin Compass 2005

1 3 5 7 9 10 8 6 4 2

LIBRARY OF CONGRESS CATALOGING IN PUBLICATION DATA
Bstan-'dzin-rgya-mtsho, Dalai Lama XIV, 1935–
Many ways to Nirvana : reflections and advice on right living / His Holiness
the Dalai Lama ; edited by Renuka Singh.
p. cm.
Contents: The four seals in Buddhism—Overcoming negative emotions—
Self-development through the six perfections—Cultivating equanimity—
The four noble truths and the eight verses of thought transformation.
ISBN 0 14 21.9637 1
1. Buddhism—Doctrines. 2. Spiritual life—Buddhism.
I. Singh, Renuka, 1953– II. Title.
BQ7935.B774M36 2005
294.3'444—dc22   2004060244

Printed in the United States of America
Set in Fournier • Designed by Victoria Hartman

*In memory of
the late Lama Yeshe
who taught that the best patience
was enlightenment
and made me taste lasting happiness.*

Contents

Acknowledgments

*I*t is a great honor to have the permission and blessings of my spiritual teachers, His Holiness Tenzin Gyatso, the Fourteenth Dalai Lama, and Venerable Lama Zopa Rinpoche, to put together the Dharma Celebration lectures once again. I would like to express thanks from the bottom of my heart for their immeasurable kindness and affection. The cooperation and help of Tenzin Geyche Tethong, Lhakdor-la, and Tenzin Taklha from His Holiness's private office is always invaluable. I am grateful to them, and also to my colleagues at Jawaharlal Nehru University for their camaraderie.

Additional thanks and gratitude to all the members associated with the Tushita Centre for their

Acknowledgments

support and advice. In particular, I am indebted to Ven. Yeshe Chodron, Dr. Jackie Tarter, Ven. Roger Kunsang, Clair Isitt, Ven. Marcel Bertels, Frances Shenker, Susie Roy, Joan Mahony, Derek Goh, Bruno Furrer, Ranjit Walia, Sunil Sud, the Chaudhrys, the Bhandaris, the Mathurs, the Jhalanis, Sadhna Kumar, and Satish Nanda.

I deeply appreciate the hard work and editorial input of my editors at Penguin, Karthika V. K. and Kalpana Joshi. Thanks also to my publisher, David Davidar, for his constant encouragement. It is always nice to have assistance from my doctoral students as well, especially Sarah Jayal Sawkmie and Meera Mohanty.

Finally, I would like to thank my father, Pritam Singh, and my family in the United States—the Pauls—for being with me through thick and thin.

—*Renuka Singh*
New Delhi
2004

Introduction

The Tushita Mahayana Meditation Centre was founded by the late Lama Yeshe and Venerable Lama Zopa Rinpoche, who is its current spiritual director. Following the tragedy that befell Tibet in the 1950s and the flight of many Tibetans to exile in India and elsewhere, our precious teacher, His Holiness the Dalai Lama, has been a spring of inspiration for all the traditions of Tibetan Buddhism that have been trying to preserve their spiritual heritage. The idea behind the Tushita Centre in Delhi, according to Lama Yeshe, is to repay the kindness of Indians for their support and generosity toward Tibetans and also to make an offering to the Arya Bhumi—the land of Lord Buddha and other spiritual masters.

This is the twenty-fifth anniversary of Tushita's existence in Delhi. Each year, Tushita sponsors the Dharma Celebration teachings in which His Holiness the Dalai Lama gives discourses on Buddhism. This was the dream of the late Lama Yeshe. Over the course of twenty-five years, we have had seventeen such celebrations.

This book is a sequel to the earlier collection of annual Dharma Celebration teachings called *Live in a Better Way*. This volume contains lectures delivered from 1999 onward, with the exception of "The Four Noble Truths and the Eight Verses of Thought Transformation," which was most likely given in the early eighties. "The Four Seals in Buddhism," "Self-Development through the Six Perfections," "Overcoming Negative Emotions," and "Cultivating Equanimity" construct as well as instruct on many ways to nirvana.

In his lectures, His Holiness uses modern perspectives to give force and clarity to what the Buddha taught 2,500 years ago. Emphasis is placed on both analysis and explication since students of Buddhism recognize it as a religion suitable for the age of reason and analysis. His Holiness also tries to connect religion to war, peace, politics, personal development, sex, ethics, media, and family life. This book is meant especially for readers who are motivated more by scientific and philosophical concerns than mere ritualistic religious interests. His Holiness simply amplifies what the Buddha said and reminds us about the significance of interfaith dialogue. Thus, in these turbulent times, people need to find the requisite motivating power and commitment within themselves, and not to exhaust their energy and time by pursuing material needs and pandering to their passion for insatiable desires.

While we have explored the depths of the seas and the skies, and ventured beyond the planet Earth, our minds—the closest pearls of wisdom—remain mysterious and unfathomable. However, 2,500 years ago, Buddha Shakyamuni, through meditation, experienced the essence of mind. He urged us to recognize our fundamental nature of luminosity so as not to fall prey to ignorance, and to develop our universal wisdom and compassion.

Despite the predictions of the mainstream European social thinkers of the nineteenth century, religion still remains a force to reckon with. Modernity has eroded some religious beliefs but it has not bred global skepticism. Against this background, this collection of lectures aims to foster understanding of Buddhism among people the world over. Additionally, as N. P. Jacobson highlights in his analysis of the contemporariness of

Buddha's thought in *Buddhism: The Religion of Analysis* (1966),

> The Buddha is like Hume in wanting to set man free from his own irrational attempts to build metaphysical scaffolding as a vantage point for perceiving the nature and destiny of almost everything about which man has ever had a persisting question. He is like Nietzsche in seeing the sad plight of human power shackled by the guilt-ridden resentment of the weak. He is like Marx and Engels in wanting to liberate man from the chimeras and myths under whose mystification he is pining away. The Buddha is like John Stuart Mill in seeing that the most powerful bonds that enslave man are not tyrants sitting astride great thrones but those subtle persuasions that rule the inner man and strip him of his integrity and independence. The Buddha is like Freud, too, in wanting to free the creative forces deep in human personality from the compulsive authoritarian controls of an ego or super-ego in which every urge to happiness is distorted, suppressed and denied. He is like Wittgenstein in wishing to alert man to the "mystification" of the human intellect by language.

The bondage and ignorance of our mind are removed by a pure heart which is refined and free from emotional afflictions and petty cravings. The state of nirvana can be attained after the strenuous practice of meditation. Meditation frees us from all our sociocultural conditioning and psychosomatic disorders. After winning inner battles by freeing oneself from emotions and desires that create egoism and attachment, the individual succeeds in transforming negative states of anxiety, disability, and depression into pure bliss and contentment. Hence, there are many ways to nirvana, that is, passage beyond sorrow.

According to Jeffrey Hopkins in *Meditation on Emptiness* (1983), a nirvana is an analytical cessation that comes into existence upon the abandonment of the last affliction. It is not the act of cessation or of passing beyond sorrow but rather a phenomenon possessed in the continuum of a yogi that is the mere absence of the ceased afflictions. Thus, the Four Noble Truths is a true path, which becomes the means of attaining true cessations.

To conclude, I quote the message of our spiritual director, Venerable Lama Zopa Rinpoche:

> The purpose of life is not just to obtain happiness and solve problems for ourselves alone; its main purpose is to free all sentient beings from every suffering and lead them all to happiness, especially the ultimate happiness of full enlightenment. This is not only the purpose of our life, it is our responsibility.

Introduction

If this is our responsibility, do we have the ability to help others find freedom from suffering and attain all happiness? Yes, we do. First, our minds have Buddha nature. Second, we have achieved the perfect human rebirth, this precious human body qualified by eight freedoms and ten richnesses.

Buddha nature is the mind's capacity to bring all happiness, temporal or ultimate, to all sentient beings, including ourselves. Our perfect human rebirth gives us every opportunity to develop our Buddha nature to its ultimate potential. Freeing all sentient beings from suffering and bringing them all happiness means liberating them from the root cause of suffering: the ignorance that abides in their mental continuum, the wrong conception of the self-existent I.

The only way we can do this is by revealing the true path: the teaching on the two truths, ultimate and conventional. This teaching explains the difference between reality and illusion. Therefore, people must listen, reflect, and meditate on the teachings that explain ultimate nature, the right view of reality. By practicing in this way, sentient beings can then sever the root of suffering: ignorance of the ultimate nature of the I and the aggregates.

In effect, all delusions and karma cease, including imprints, putting a permanent end to beginningless suffering—the cycle of aging, sickness, death, and rebirth in the six realms—and achieving the everlasting happiness of nirvana, the state beyond sorrow. Subsequently, through one's gradual eradication of the subtle obscurations to omniscience comes the attainment of the peerless state of fully enlightened Buddhahood, the great nirvana.

For our spiritual advancement, we must seek teachings from a fully qualified teacher, such as His Holiness the Dalai Lama, who himself has already actualized all these paths, in particular renunciation, bodhicitta, and the right view of emptiness.

Therefore, it gives me great pleasure to know that the Dharma Celebration teachings by His Holiness the Dalai Lama have been put together once again in the form of a book.

It is my hope that this book, with its many ways to nirvana, may help people to make sense of the fragmented reality of contemporary life.

—*Renuka Singh*

*Many Ways
to Nirvana*

The Four Seals
in Buddhism

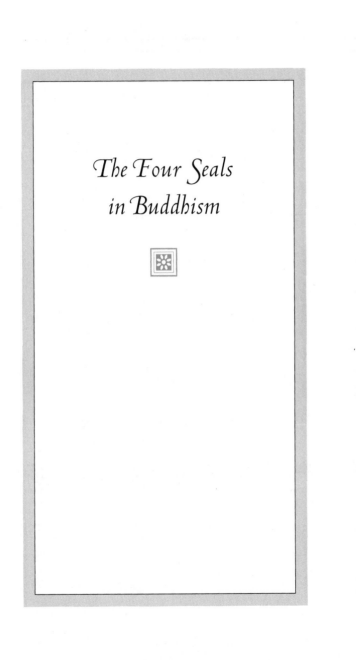

The four Buddhist seals or axioms form an important part of our religious teachings. Relevant to our time is also the training and peace of the mind. The Buddhist method of transforming the mind is not only a matter of faith but is also a conviction gained through analytical meditation. So, investigation is very essential.

In order to carry out an investigation in this regard, you need a skeptical attitude. You do not just accept issues on blind faith. Skepticism brings questions, and questions call for an investigation. The investigation is an analytical meditation through which we gain a clearer awareness: a clearer picture of reality. This produces sound conviction. It is only through sound conviction that mental transformation can take place.

In other words, our head or brain is like a laboratory. Human intelligence is unique and is different from other species of mammals. Such intelligence is an instrument. So, in the laboratory of the brain, human intelligence or intellectual capacity is used as an instrument to examine the various emotions, and then carry out experiments on an emotional level. This enables us to transform our emotions.

According to some scientists, emotion is not necessarily negative. Emotion is a very strong feeling. While some emotions are destructive, others are constructive. In a meeting with scientists, we concluded that there are emotions even in the Buddha's mind. There is a strong sense of caring and compassion and also the realization of emptiness.

In the beginning, there is just a vague feeling of emptiness. At that level, there is no emotion, but once you become more familiar with it, then that feeling increases. At a certain level, the realization of emptiness also becomes a kind of emotion. Therefore, in the practice of developing wisdom and loving-kindness/compassion, you strengthen these inner qualities and then reach a state where you have an upsurge of feeling called emotion. We can clearly see this link between intellect and emotions. Thus, the brain and heart can go side by side. I think this is the Buddhist approach.

In ancient traditions of Indian thought, similar methods have been adopted. What is unique to Buddhism is that the Buddha gave us the freedom to question his own words. Buddha clearly said that all Bhikshus and wise men should examine his words just like a goldsmith checks gold by polishing, cutting, and putting it in fire. He asked people not to accept his teachings out of sheer faith.

So there is a link between academic knowledge and actual experience. They go together. It seems to me that every major country has a religious tradition. There are two aspects to religion: one is the training of the mind, and the other is a philosophical one. In terms of training the mind, all major religions are the same. They all have the same potential to transform the human mind. A clear indication of this is that all major religious traditions carry the message of love, compassion, forgiveness, contentment, and self-discipline. The message is the same, but in some cases the meaning may be a little different because of their different philosophies.

There may be major differences in the philosophy of different religions but we cannot say that one religion is better than the other. They all have the same potential to transform the mind. However, each of us has a different mental disposition. So you see there are different methods to approach it. Nevertheless, the result or the effectiveness is more or less the same.

Therefore, we cannot say this or that religion is better. Such an attitude allows us to develop respect toward all other major religious traditions. Millions of people have been inspired by different major traditions in the past. It can help them to lead a meaningful life. In the future, millions of people will continue to be inspired and, as a result, their lives will also become more meaningful and filled with compassion. On the philosophical side, however, we can say that this philosophy is more complex or that philosophy is simpler.

In Tibetan, we talk about the four Buddhist seals or axioms. These are: all conditioned phenomena are impermanent; all contaminated phenomena are suffering; all phenomena are selfless and empty; and nirvana is peace.

To explain the first seal that all conditioned phenomena are impermanent, we must first understand that its basis is related to impermanence. Any particular phenomenon that is dependent on its causes and conditions for its existence is categorized as a conditioned phenomenon. This is subject to causes and conditions. For example, while sitting in a particular tent, we are aware that there is no tree. Because of this absence of "tree," we can know that the tree is nonexistent. In this way, our mind can know something; namely, the nonexistence of the tree. So this clearly proves that the nonexistence of the tree is actually existent because it is the subject of our knowledge.

Simultaneously, the nonexistence of the "tree" is obviously not existent in a physical sense so that we can see or perceive it. Also, it is definitely a perceivable object and, in fact, many of the things that we posit have to be made in terms of understanding the nonexistence of the tree. For example, take the flowers that you can see. One of the qualities we find in flowers is the nonexistence of the tree. It is because of this, that on this particular flower, we find the infinite existence of the nonexistences of other objects not being the flower. It is certain that the nonexistence of these other objects on this particular flower is definitely a cognizable object. But, at the same time, it is not the kind of object that can be characterized.

Similarly, in the case of objects such as impermanence or selflessness, they can be perceived and cognized by the mind but, simultaneously, do not have an existence empowered from their side.

In the same way, when we talk about generality and particularity, rather than thinking of individual flowers, we can think about a "flower" in its general sense. For example, you might see a particular flower in a particular place at a particular time. Then later on, after a certain period of time, you see a different flower of a different color. By simply seeing that second flower, you are able to conclude that this is also a flower. So, when we designate the term "flower," to what particular object do we designate that term?

If the term "flower" is designated only to that particular flower which you saw earlier, obviously that particular flower is not found in the flower that you see later on. Thus, there is a kind of "flower" which is a common quality of these two flowers. However, even though this is the reality, it does not mean that there is a common "flower" which pervades all of them and which exists as different from these flowers.

Therefore, when you notice a particular flower, you are observing a quality which is different from those objects that are not flowers. That same quality is also found in the flower which you see later. It is because of this quality that you are able to understand, perceive, and differentiate these different types of objects as "flowers."

Now the question arises: is such a phenomenon conditioned or caused? All existing phenomena can be divided into two categories: existent phenomena and nonexistent objects. When we talk about an existent phenomenon, it is determined in the sense that there is a consciousness which comprehends it, which perceives it. In the case of a nonexistent phenomenon or object, it is something that is not perceived or cognized by any type of consciousness.

We are not implying here that anything that is perceived by any type of mind does exist. So, again, we have to make a distinct classification between different types of mind: valid mind or invalid mind. It is because of this that when you study Buddhist epistemology, you find different types of minds described.

Regarding the actual meaning of valid cognition, there are scholars who give a similar kind of definition and agree upon the meaning of valid cognition. However, there are divergent viewpoints. Great masters like Dignaga and Dharmakirti explain these points in great detail.

There are vast differences or varieties or types

within the meaning of causes and conditions. But, primarily, we have two kinds of causes. The first is called a substantial cause—a cause that is primarily responsible for bringing into function, on production, the nature of a particular object, the entity of a particular object. The second is what we call the cooperative condition, which is an existing factor for the coming into existence of that particular object.

Therefore, within the universe of mind, whether it is a positive or a negative mind, a positive or a negative emotion, in both cases, there are two main causes. These are, first, the substantial cause which is responsible for the production of the entity of that very nature of the mind, and second, the cooperative cause which is a kind of circumstantial factor which gives a particular mind the opportunity to arise.

Aryadeva, in his four hundred verses, clearly said that negative or afflictive emotions which arise from a substantial cause are difficult to extinguish. However, negative emotions which arise from cooperative conditions or circumstantial factors are easier to handle. Dependent on immediate circumstances and factors, they can be subdued and eliminated. Examples of these emotions are hatred, anger, attachment, and, on the positive side, compassion and a sense of caring.

Familiarity with these emotions causes them to rise again. These are sound. Emotions that come into existence because of encountering a circumstance, whether positive or negative, are not very sound.

Of course, there are other types of factors and conditions. All kinds of phenomena, which are dependent and produced by causes and their conditions, are known as conditioned or impermanent phenomena. Basically, there are two levels of meaning of impermanence: impermanence in the grosser level, and impermanence in its subtler nature of existence. The grosser level of impermanence refers to transitory states of a particular object in the sense of disintegration of its continuity. When we talk about subtle impermanence, it is more in the sense of momentary disintegration rather than disintegration in terms of its continuity.

When we say all conditioned phenomena are impermanent, we are referring to the subtler level of impermanence: the momentary disintegration of a particular object. This subtler level of impermanence can be understood in two ways: first, the nonexistence of the first moment of impermanent phenomena during the second moment, and second, the very first moment of that impermanent phenomenon which is produced in such a way that it is the cause of the phenomenon's disintegration.

How do we prove and how do we know that there is this moment-by-moment disintegration at the subtle level? We do this through understanding the grosser level of impermanence, namely, the disintegration of a particular conditioned phenomenon in terms of its continuity. For example, we see a mountain crumbling, a house collapsing, and so forth. By knowing this disintegration of the continuity of a particular object, we conclude that there is a subtle change going on. Unless a subtle level of change occurs, it is not possible for that object to undergo a grosser level of change.

Even in the case of a rock, which we normally see as something solid, something that appears unchanging, when we look into the nature of that particular rock at its subatomic level, we see that it is constantly undergoing changes. This, in short, is the meaning that all conditioned phenomena are impermanent.

Clearly, the first moment of a conditioned phenomenon is produced in this state of disintegration. The production is the cause of the disintegration. It does not need a new cause for the disintegration of a particular object. In short, the Sautantrika, the Cittamatra, and the Madhyamika Buddhist schools of thought accept that the disintegration of a particular conditioned phenomenon is not dependent on a fresh cause for its disintegration. The Vaibhashika school has a slightly different explanation.

Therefore, we say the impermanent phenomena are "other-powered," or dependent on their causes. A cause, which is the producer of a particular effect, is, in turn, dependent on a cause which produces it. So, any cause which is a producer of a result is, in turn, a result of its own cause. That kind of pervasion is there. Pervasion means that all producing causes are always the result of their own causes. Therefore, the cause/effect relationship or law of causality is a continuous circle.

When we see that the law of causality functions, we can distinguish two kinds of objects which experience this cause/effect relationship. These are the realm of the physical body and that of the mind. What distinguishes these two realms are the substantial causes that determine them. The substantial cause of the mind, or what is responsible for the production of a mind, must be a mind, not a physical body. That substantial cause distinguishes the mind from a physical object.

In terms of cooperative conditions, there could be a mind that acts as a cooperative condition for the production of a physical object. Similarly, there could be a physical object that acts as a cooperative condition for the production of a mind. There could also be an object that is dependent on its causes and conditions but when we talk about that object's nature, then it depends on the conceptual thought which designates that particular object. In other words, the identification of that particular object is dependent on the designating mind.

The second of the four axioms or Buddhist seals is that all contaminated phenomena are in the nature of suffering. The "contamination" here primarily refers to the afflictive emotions or negative emotions and the imprints or predispositions of these afflictive emotions. However, here we should primarily understand the contaminating factor as the afflictive emotions rather than the imprints. When we say all contaminated things are suffering, we mean those objects which are either produced by afflictive emotions or are dependent on them.

To understand how all contaminated phenomena are in the nature of suffering, we have to understand the three levels of suffering. First, there is the suffering of suffering, then there is the suffering of change, and, finally, there is conditioned suffering. When we talk about all contaminated phenomena as suffering, we refer to the third level of suffering: conditioned suffering. This acts as the foundation for the other two levels of suffering.

We can try to understand how all contaminated phenomena are in the nature of suffering by examining the law of causality. Earlier, I explained that all conditioned phenomena are dependent on their respective causes and conditions. The mere fact of depending on causes and conditions produces afflictive emotions. Those are, by definition, in the nature of suffering.

The third axiom states that all phenomena are empty and selfless. Here, we mean all phenomena, and not merely conditioned phenomena. We are not merely talking about those phenomena that are dependent on causes and conditions, but mean both permanent phenomena and impermanent phenomena.

What do we mean when we say that all phenomena are empty and selfless? There are divergent viewpoints about this among the four Buddhist schools of thought. The meaning of selflessness that is commonly accepted by all Buddhist schools of thought (except a few of the eighteen subschools of the Vaibhashikas) is the absence of a person that is independent and substantially existent.

When we examine Buddhist and non-Buddhist philosophical viewpoints, non-Buddhist schools affirm the notion of a person as independent and substantially existent. But the Buddhist schools refute this view. Those who accept a person as independent and substantially existent also assert that there is a kind of soul which exists separately from the physical and mental aggregates (the body and mind). They add that this kind of soul or person comes from the previous life into this one and then goes on to the next life. All Buddhist schools of thought refute the existence of such a self.

If such an independent, substantially existent self or soul exists, we should be able to pinpoint it. Upon investigation, we should be able to find such a person or soul. Furthermore, if the self is permanent, particularly in the sense of a person who is independent and substantially existent, we cannot refer to the disintegration of that self, the aging of that self, because it is asserted that it is totally independent from the psychophysical aggregates and is permanent. The Vaibhashika and Sautantrika schools of thought refer only to the selflessness of a person and not of a phenomenon.

The Prasangika Madhyamika and Cittamatra schools of thought have a higher perspective. They say that an autonomous and substantially existent person does not exist. By adopting this philosophical notion, one can definitely reduce craving, grasping, and attachment.

However, this view will not attack the grasping at the psychophysical aggregates. Therefore, when you ascend to the higher Buddhist schools of thought, they talk not only of the lack of existence of an independent, substantially existent person, but also of the selflessness of phenomena. They assert the lack of an independent existence of the psychophysical aggregates.

Regarding the meaning of selflessness of phenomena, there are differences between the Mind-Only (Cittamatra) school and the Middle Way (Madhyamika) school. When the Mind-Only school refers to selflessness of phenomena, it means the subject lacks substantial separateness. It refutes an externally existent object but asserts the independent existence of the mind, the perceiver. So, by meditating on this view of the Mind-Only school, one can reduce grasping and craving toward the external object.

For the Madhyamikas, the Mind-Only school does not solve the problem. If one adopts the

Mind-Only view, one may be able to reduce craving and grasping toward an externally existent object but different kinds of negative and strong mental emotions will arise. This is because the Mind-Only school asserts the independent or inherent existence of the mind.

Therefore, for the Madhyamikas, there is no counterforce to these emotions in the view of the Mind-Only school. Instead, from the Madhyamika viewpoint, as regards external objects and the internal mind, the perceiver is the same. They are equal in terms of having no inherent existence or absolute objective existence.

Thus, when we say that all phenomena are empty and selfless, we should become familiar with the different levels of presentation by the philosophical schools. In fact, when each of these four Buddhist schools of thought makes its presentation of the meaning of selflessness or emptiness, they each cite quotations from Buddha's own teachings.

For example, in certain sutras, it appears that the particular sutra is talking about a person that is independent and substantially existent. There is a statement in a sutra that the five psychophysical aggregates are the loads or burdens, and the person is the one who carries these loads or burdens. So, it appears as if the person and the psychophysical aggregates are separate.

Now the question arises, if all these presentations by the four Buddhist schools of thought are derived from the sutra sources, with sutra quotations, how do we conclude which one is correct? For this, we need to rely upon logic and reason. We can prove through our understanding and perception that the philosophical presentation of the higher Buddhist schools of thought is more logical than the lower schools. One might have a subtle understanding of the meaning of selflessness so that a person has no independent or substantial existence, but one can still have a wrong understanding of the philosophical viewpoint. A practitioner can have thoroughly understood the lack of a substantial separateness of the subject and object, but may still strongly grasp at seeing the mind as inherently existent.

Once you have a thorough understanding of the philosophical viewpoint presented by the Madhyamika school of thought, then you are able to see both the subject (the mind) and the object as having no inherent, absolute, or objective existence. While you have that kind of understanding, it is impossible to have misconceptions about the self, as presented in the lower Buddhist schools of thought, arise.

By using this kind of analysis and investigation, we are able to conclude that the meaning of self-lessness or emptiness propounded by the higher Buddhist schools of thought is much more profound. So, that is the meaning of "all phenomena are empty and selfless."

From the philosophical viewpoint of the Vaibhashika, when they talk about the lack of existence of a person that has an independent or substantial existence and they say that all phenomena are self-less, they do not refer to it as presented by the higher Buddhist schools. As the Vaibhashikas talk about the nonexistence of a person which is substantially existent and independent, they conclude that there is no object that can be enjoyed by such a person. On the basis of this reasoning, they assert that all phenomena are selfless.

From the Madhyamika viewpoint, this meaning of the selflessness of all phenomena is a superficial explanation. It lacks depth because one can talk about selflessness of phenomena only by relating it specifically to the nonexistence of an independent and substantially existent person. Therefore, one cannot talk of the selflessness of an object without relating it to the selflessness of the person.

In contrast, the Madhyamika school accepts the existence of an external object. So, for them, the meaning of selflessness presented by the Mind-Only school is something that is made up by the mind. It is not the correct meaning. The Mind-Only school only talks about the lack of existence of the external object and not of the mind. For the Madhyamikas, it is a fabricated viewpoint because it does not conform to the reality, and therefore is not a valid finding.

For the Madhyamikas, the Mind-Only viewpoint is not based on a solid foundation or a valid cognition. Even if you try to practice meditation and make yourself familiar with the concepts of emptiness and selflessness, you cannot develop your mind to a limitless state. For this reason, the viewpoint or the meaning of emptiness or selflessness should not be superficial (as presented by the Vaibhashika schools) nor should it just be mentally fabricated (as in the Mind-Only school).

The fourth axiom is "nirvana is peace." A literal translation of the Tibetan usage is "transcendence of suffering is peace." Here, transcendence of the dissatisfied state refers to afflictive emotions. It is only once you transcend the influence of afflictive emotions that you are able to achieve permanent peace and happiness. Therefore, nirvana is peace. However, in terms of the actual meaning of the nature or entity of nirvana, there are divergent viewpoints. According to Nagarjuna, nirvana refers to the state of cessation of afflictive emotions. When the mind is totally purified of afflictive emotions, that state of the mind is called nirvana.

So, that is just a brief introduction to the meaning of the four axioms or Buddhist seals. Now the question is: how can this philosophical thought be applied to the actual transformation and training of the mind?

In our daily life, many of our unruly, disturbing, negative thoughts arise because of four kinds of misconceptions. First, we tend to see what is impermanent as permanent; second, we tend to comprehend what is unclean as clean and as something which has an essence or meaning; third, we are inclined to see those who are selfless as having self-existence; and fourth, we are likely to view what is in the nature of suffering as a source of happiness and peace.

Even at the ordinary, conventional level, there are people who are more farsighted than others, who are more concerned with long-term rather than short-term interests. When we find some contradiction between long-term and short-term interests, we prefer long-term interests. We can sacrifice short-term interests. As a result of pursuing these long-term interests, there is more suffering.

For example, the greedy want more and more. Such a person is completely ignorant about the capacity of his body to use wealth. The body itself has a limited capacity to consume things. Perhaps this is a silly example, but even a billionaire has a stomach which is of normal size and can consume only a certain amount of food. Then, if you take ornaments or rings, even a billionaire only has ten fingers! If you put a diamond ring on each finger, the maximum you can wear is just ten. If you put two or three rings on each finger, it looks very ugly, doesn't it?

Therefore, persons who want more and more, unfortunately, always go on trying to obtain more wealth in order to use things. Furthermore, they never think of death or the limitation of our body and our life. So this way of life, of accumulating wealth continuously, makes you feel that just as you have stored and accumulated wealth, similarly your life will go on continuously without encountering death and you will be able to enjoy this wealth forever.

When you go on accumulating wealth and acquisitions with a lack of contentment, what is the result? You do not relax physically or get mental peace or time to rest. I think that the very reason we seek more wealth and power is to get some kind of satisfaction. Unless you have a proper mental attitude, you are just seeking some sort of satisfaction.

This way, we will never reach any satisfaction, and something will always be wrong. Such people do not have mental happiness or stability. Normally, we aspire to and appreciate the life of a billionaire but if we look closer at their mental state, they have a lot of worry, anxiety, jealousy, and other painful things. Worst of all, because of the discontentment, sometimes they do not hesitate to use wrong methods or harm or exploit others. So what is the result? Eventually, you make more enemies and earn a bad name. You will not get satisfaction in the end because of this desire. You will have to die with a bad reputation.

Another problem is the increasing gap between the rich and the poor at the global level as well as the national level. While some people have luxurious lifestyles and are wasting millions, others living on the same planet are hungry and some are even starving. This is a very difficult situation. And what is the result of this gap? Apart from the mental suffering, there is more crime, unrest, and physical violence. This huge gap between the rich and the poor is not only morally wrong but is also a source of many problems.

To address these problems, one needs to meditate on impermanence and the suffering nature of samsara. The very existence of this body, the existence of our life, is actually under the influence or control of our afflictive emotions. Once we realize that suffering is the very nature of existence, it helps to reduce our unreasonable desire for things.

Therefore, the concept of emptiness is a crucial factor. If we analyze this concept properly and experiment with it, especially when we become involved in strong negative emotions, then the object (whether colored by hatred, attachment, or jealousy) appears as something very solid. At the particular moment when we develop such strong negative emotions, we tend to see that specific object in one of two ways. On the one hand, we see it as something extremely interesting, beautiful, and existing from its own side. On the other, we tend to see it as being totally negative and ugly, with that kind of ugliness and negativity existing from its own side.

Therefore, because of these afflictive emotions, we tend to grasp strongly at that particular object. In some cases, practicing compassion can indirectly reduce an afflictive emotion, but we cannot directly fight them. Instead, we can use the wisdom which understands ultimate reality: emptiness. Only this kind of understanding and feeling has an effect on these negative emotions. Of course, we can learn this only through our direct experience.

Eventually, we will generate a feeling that it is possible to eliminate these afflictive emotions. We do this by understanding and meditating on shamatha. That mental state, where all afflictive emotions are completely annihilated, is called nirvana. If you meditate properly, understanding and linking all these philosophical topics, this can be used to develop some kind of conviction.

It is in this context that the Buddha taught the Four Noble Truths. If you meditate on the first two truths of suffering and its causes, your anxiety and sadness increase. But you see the Buddha did not stop there. There are two more truths: cessation of suffering and the path or method to achieve that cessation. Buddha began by explaining that the very nature of our existence is suffering, but at the same time, he also showed that there is an alternative.

So, the main purpose of meditating on suffering is to cultivate a determination to achieve nirvana. If there is no possibility to achieve nirvana, it is better not to think about suffering and, instead, just take it easy, drink alcohol, or whatever you like. That would be much better. However, if there is an alternative, a possibility to eliminate these troublesome states of mind or emotions, it really is worthwhile to make an effort. That is how to train the mind.

The practice of compassion, having a sense of concern for others, is immensely beneficial to oneself. Of course, eventually, other sentient beings will also benefit. Therefore, as Lama Tsongkhapa correctly says, when you develop compassion and altruism, your main focus is to benefit and help others, but it is you who will derive the greatest benefit.

Thus, practicing and meditating on loving-kindness and compassion fulfils the purpose of your life and that of other sentient beings. Such practice and meditation, which makes your mind familiar with the cultivation of loving-kindness and compassion, is not something that should be limited only to believers. Even for nonbelievers, it is extremely important to develop such habits and positive qualities of the mind. It brings you happiness and the happiness or peace of other sentient beings. It is all interrelated and depends on the development of loving-kindness and compassion.

Practicing compassion, caring for others and sharing their problems, lays the foundation of a happy life not only at the level of the individual, family, or community but also for humanity as a whole. So, the promotion of these basic human values is very important. Also, it is a responsibility for everyone because the future of humanity is entirely in our hands.

As Buddhists, we believe in prayers, meditation, and blessings from higher beings. There are higher beings who have the power of blessing but the effect is limited. There are countless buddhas and bodhisattvas who always pray for us, but, nevertheless, our condition remains quite difficult! We are still in samsara.

So I always tell my brothers and sisters that action is more important than prayer. We must make an effort. Sometimes, I feel that my talk about compassion is merely paying lip service. I really admire those individuals or organizations that are involved in helping impoverished people and working in the area of education, and so on. These people are implementing compassion on a practical level. I just sit here on a comfortable seat and talk about compassion! Perhaps this is hypocrisy.

So action is very important. In order to be able to implement an action tirelessly, we need a firm determination. We should have a clear vision about our goal. This will enable us to make the effort naturally and tirelessly. If the goal is not very clear, or there is some obscurity in it, then obscure methods will be used and this creates even more confusion!

These complicated philosophical concepts should not result in our taking a zigzag approach to life. Instead, through the study of these philosophical concepts, we can develop a clear picture or map. Then we know how to go about things.

Lastly, we would like to generate the mind of enlightenment. Normally, this is done by first collecting merit and purifying negativities by doing the seven-limbed practice.

Many of us belong to different traditions. Perhaps we can imagine all the other ancient masters like Jesus Christ or Mahavir. We can visualize them and promise to serve and help other sentient beings. In this way, our lives will become meaningful.

Just to strive for one's survival is not enough. Even plants have the capacity to survive. Similarly, animals and insects have some kind of instinct for their survival. But we humans have this marvelous intelligence. To use this merely for one's survival is a waste. Instead, this gift of intelligence should be used for altruism. Then our life will really become meaningful.

From the Buddhist viewpoint, our life on this planet lasts for a maximum of a hundred years. It is like a tourist vacation. From the depths of mysterious space, we arrive here to stay for just a hundred years. When you compare that to the billions and billions of light-years we have existed, a hundred years is insignificant!

So, to use your short human life to create more trouble and pain does not make sense. If an American or a European tourist came to India for just a week and during that week created trouble wherever he or she went, that would be pointless and foolish. Similarly, we have come to this planet for a short visit. So this time should be used meaningfully. This means helping others wherever possible. If you cannot help others, do not create pain or suffering for others.

To generate the mind of enlightenment, I would like us to read these three verses three times together:

> With a wish to free all beings
> I shall always go for refuge
> To the Buddha, Dharma, and Sangha
> Until I reach full enlightenment.

Enthused by wisdom and compassion
Today in the Buddha's presence
I generate the mind for full awakening
For the benefit of all sentient beings.

As long as space remains
As long as sentient beings remain
Until then, may I too remain
And dispel the miseries of the world.

People who want to practice altruism (and, of course, Buddhists) should read this as part of their daily prayer. They should meditate upon it, especially the last verse. All three verses are part of my daily prayer and meditation. Every day, I repeat and meditate on these lines. The last one is very powerful. When I get into an unhappy mood or have negative afflictive emotions, then I remember this. I recite this and then contemplate on it. This immediately restores my peace of mind. It is very helpful. Even non-Buddhists can think about the last sentence.

Your Holiness, why did Shakyamuni Buddha remain silent for one week after he became enlightened?

There is a story of Buddha remaining silent and not giving the teachings for seven weeks. Buddha is supposed to have said, "I have found a teaching, a path that is profound, peaceful, free from elaborations, unconditioned. I have found a teaching that is like nectar. But if I try to explain and teach this to others, nobody will be able to understand it. Therefore, I will remain silent and retire into the forest." At that time, there was no media available so nobody was able to announce Buddha's enlightenment! Buddha's enlightenment was not widely known. Therefore, after his enlightenment, there was a great delay. Gradually, more and more people became aware that Shakyamuni Buddha had some kind of special experiences. Then some people began to receive teachings from him and to ask him questions.

Can you fully describe consciousness?

The only way to know consciousness fully is through experience. Sometimes I use one particular method. I just try to stay in the "thoughtlessness" state of mind and then, eventually I get some kind of empty feeling. If one stays there, eventually one will experience total clarity and purity. From that state of clarity and purity, one can also go through various experiences and appearances. Therefore, this kind of mere experiential and luminous nature of the mind can be understood through repeated and continuous practice of meditation. It is something that cannot simply be explained in words.

Is substantial cause the same as karma? How do we break out of the cycle of karma?

Unless you are able to put an end to the ignorance which is the first of the twelve links of dependent origination, it is not possible for us to put an end to karma. Even for a realized being such as an arhat (who has totally destroyed all afflictive emotions), a residue of karma remains. In this context, in the *Pramanavarttika*, it is said that one who has transcended the cycle of existence (samsara), one who has transcended the desire and craving within the cycle of existence, such a person is able to get out of samsara. This is because such a person has extinguished all afflictive emotions. Once you have done that, there is no prime cause for the accumulation of contaminated actions.

Is it possible to gain enlightenment in a woman's body?

Oh, certainly. There are some differences. There are also different interpretations according to Buddhist schools of thought, including the Yoga Tantra and the sutra teachings. The first principle of enlightenment should always be on the basis of a male being and not a female. However, according to the highest Buddhist system, Maha Anuttarayoga Tantra, it is possible even for women to become enlightened. So, of course, we regard that as the ultimate or final explanation.

If there is no self, what or who is going from life to life?

When Buddhists talk about selflessness, it does not mean we deny the existence of self, but deny self as something permanent and unchanging. Buddhists deny that kind of self exists. For Buddhists, the self is only designated on the continuation of mind. The mind is beginningless and endless. Therefore, self is also beginningless and endless. From beginninglessness it goes up to Buddhahood. The self is still there even at the Buddhahood level. Nagarjuna says that even in mahaparinirvana, the self is still there, the Buddha is still there, and the Buddha mind is also there.

I am not satisfied by your answers. Is this also a kind of greed?

That's not greed.

Do you believe in angels?

Angels have a different form of life and are a different kind of spirit. We do believe in dakinis, and if dakinis are considered to be angels, there are a lot of dakinis.

What connects mind/body or body/mind?

The grosser level of mind. The grosser level of mind occurs because of the body. It no longer exists when the body ceases to function. But, at a more subtle level, a different kind of mind or consciousness remains. For example, when you awake from sleep, there is a certain level of consciousness, a certain level of mind that functions. When we are sleeping, whether it is deep sleep or a sleep with dreams, a certain level of mind or consciousness still functions.

Furthermore, in deep sleep, without dreaming, another level of mind exists. When you faint and you are not breathing, it becomes more subtle.

The most subtle level of mind occurs when we die. Once the heartbeat stops and the brain stops functioning, then the most subtle mind of all manifests. An indication of this are those individuals who are declared dead medically, yet whose bodies do not decay and remain fresh. In some cases, the body remains so for two to three weeks. We believe that the subtle mind is still there in the body and because of this, the body does not decay.

Thus, there are many different levels of mind. Some depend heavily on this body while others are more or less independent of it.

What comes after nirvana?

It depends on what kind of nirvana you have actualized. For example, if you have actualized a kind of nirvana that is merely the cessation of afflictive emotions, you still have to achieve enlightenment or Buddhahood.

How can we overcome hatred?

The most important practice in this connection is to think about the disadvantages of negativity or hatred. It is through this kind of analysis that you will be able to understand the benefits of not devel-

oping hate. When we talk about overcoming hatred, it can be understood at two levels: first, not allowing an opportunity for hatred to arise in our
day-to-day life, and second, thinking about the destructive nature and results of hatred.

By contemplating in this way, you will be able
to distance yourself and not allow hatred to arise
in your daily life. In order to uproot or totally
eliminate hatred, you have to enter into deeper
spiritual practices. These are primarily the practice
of achieving a one-pointed mind, which is also
called a mind of "calm abiding," and gaining a
deeper insight into emptiness or ultimate reality.

Usually, I ask: what's the benefit of these negative emotions such as hatred and jealousy? They
are harmful for one's peace of mind. These are our
real enemies. External enemies have the ability to
attack us and destroy our peace of mind in a limited way. External enemies cannot destroy our
peace of mind, but as soon as an emotion such as
hatred arises, this internal enemy takes away our
peace of mind.

Also, such internal enemies harm our health.
For example, three years ago I met some scientists
in New York. A medical scientist made a presentation where he made it clear that those people who
use the words "me," "mine," and "I" frequently

are more at risk of suffering from a heart attack. This is quite simple.

The moment we think of ourselves—me—we are very self-centered and narrow-minded. Our area of operation becomes very small. Under such circumstances, even small problems appear to loom large, be unbearable, and generate more worry and anxiety. On the other hand, the moment one thinks about the welfare of other beings, one's mind automatically widens.

In Buddhist practice, one thinks about the infinite sentient beings and their problems and suffering, not only the first or the second types of suffering but also the third type. Because of this, one becomes more understanding and concerned and one's mind becomes more spacious. Thus, one's problem becomes insignificant.

One's mental attitude and outlook make a big difference. Afflictive emotions are harmful for one's health and these negative emotions actively thrive within our minds. Such a person always creates problems wherever he or she goes. On the other hand, a person with peace of mind or a compassionate mind will have more friends. Wherever that person goes, there is a peaceful atmosphere. Even the animals appreciate it.

The purpose of our life is to feel happiness, joy,

satisfaction, and peace. In order to achieve that, so much depends on our mental attitude rather than money, power, or external things. So try and analyze these things. This is the best way to transform our mental attitude.

If you care for your family more than for other sentient beings, is that being selfish?

There are two kinds of caring. If you just think of your family exclusively and do not bother about other sentient beings, that is attachment. But if you practice caring for all sentient beings, your family too becomes a part of these sentient beings. Also, you can communicate directly on this basis when you are taking care of your family members. You include even yourself, right?

It is necessary and good. In fact, sometimes when we pray, we want to benefit all sentient beings, except our neighbor! So we have to fight! Praying only for those sentient beings who are very far away is a mistake. When we pray for all sentient beings, our action reaches family members or neighbors in the first place. So, pray for your neighbor; you can then correctly say that you are really practicing for the benefit of all sentient beings.

As a teacher, how can I teach children about love and compassion?

Through your action! Through your example—not merely your words. So you should think and develop a genuine concern about their welfare, their long-term future. You can explain to students about the value of a sense of caring, compassion, and tolerance. A very important concept is that of dialogue, the spirit of dialogue, and reconciliation because in human society there are always conflicts and contradictions.

Contradiction itself is good. For example, the Four Noble Truths are also contradictions—so contradictions can bring about more development. On the other hand, contradictions can be negative and lead to conflict, bloodshed, and fighting. Education is a very important way to provide knowledge and awareness along with basic human values.

Is emptiness the same as selflessness?

Perhaps the word "emptiness" has a wider connotation because when we use the word "selflessness," it can refer not only to the lack of the inherent existence of an object but also to the lack of a self-cherishing attitude.

Your Holiness, what message do you have for the new millennium?

If we review the last century, we see that a lot of change has taken place on this planet. Some changes were positive, while others were negative. Anyway, I believe that because of their different experiences, humanity as a whole is becoming more mature. I think our minds are more open. Also, we have a better awareness of the long-term consequences of our actions, including the effect on the ecology. So there is hope for a better future. It depends entirely on our actions.

Constitution Club Lawns, 1999

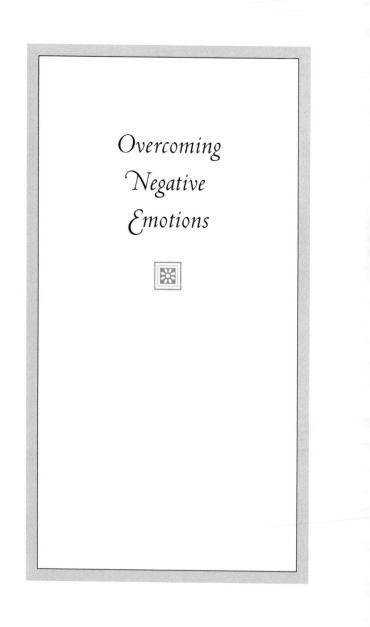

Overcoming
Negative
Emotions

When I look at myself, over the years, the physical body has changed. Day by day, we are all getting older, but our knowledge is also increasing. And our experience is increasing. But gaining knowledge is much easier than implementing that knowledge. The implementation, the practice, is not easy. For myself, also, it is difficult. However, when I compare my way of thinking today with what it was twenty years ago, I think that there is some change, some progress. It doesn't matter how much, as long as there is some.

In a way, change or progress or transformation of the mind is easy, in a way, difficult. But one thing is quite clear: I can assure you that if you make an effort constantly with determination and conviction, the mind can change. Therefore, even if you think that little progress is being made, there is sufficient reason to continue to try, because slowly, slowly, you are changing. Even if you are unable to bring about a dramatic change, even if you are able to achieve a minimum of change, that is still a change. In the Buddha Dharma, and in some ancient Hindu traditions, we believe in rebirth, life after life. So in this lifetime, if we develop in the spiritual field, even a limited progress will make an impact on our next life. Then another attempt can be made. The little progress will certainly carry a positive effect on our coming lives.

So that is why Buddha Shakyamuni tells us that a practitioner should think in terms of eons, not just days and hours. Our life, from a Buddhist viewpoint, has no beginning. The desire to overcome suffering, right from the beginning, is there. But that desire alone does not achieve the goal. Along with that desire, we have to follow the right method, the proper method. We have to make the effort tirelessly, irrespective of the years or eons. Then, there will be an end to our suffering. Buddha demonstrated this very clearly.

Perhaps the majority of us, according to the Tibetan Buddhist tradition, believe that the recitation of *Om Mani Pedme Hung* is good for living beings, especially those people who are facing adverse situations. So here, at the beginning, let us recite one hundred times *Om Mani Pedme Hung* for the people who have suffered in the Gujarat earthquake.

According to today's newspaper, more than twenty thousand people have perished in the earthquake. Think of those people who died or were injured or lost their family members. Think also of the animals. No doubt, cats, dogs, and other animals have also suffered.

So, remember all those sentient beings, particularly human beings, and those poor people who, even while they lived, had difficult lives, and at the end died tragically. It is very sad, isn't it?

Now I want to share with you some feelings, views, and experiences of my visit to the Kumbha Mela festival. I spent two days there. Actually, this was not my first visit: in 1966, I visited another Kumbha Mela. That time, my stay was very short, with no opportunity to talk privately with spiritual leaders. So this time, in addition to the public functions, I got the opportunity to have discussions with the shankaracharya and some other gurus.

When I first visited the Kumbha Mela in 1966, I received some letters from a Buddhist group expressing their resentment about my visit to what was regarded as a Hindu festival. This time also, some of my friends expressed a little reservation about my visit there. Then I thought, and I think people know, of my interest and commitment to the promotion of human values and religious harmony. These two commitments I will carry till my death.

For more than fifteen years, whenever I have had an opportunity, I have made pilgrimages to the holy places of different religious traditions like Jerusalem, and Lourdes in France. In India also, when I am near a place with well-known shrines, mosques, temples, or churches, I pay my respects. I felt that attending the Kumbha Mela was a good opportunity to show my respect to the ancient Indian religion Hinduism. I have stayed in this country for forty-one years and have always felt it important to show my respect for other traditions and to learn about them. I include those traditions too which are alien to India, like Christianity, Islam, Judaism, and those traditions which have grown within this country, like Hinduism, Jainism, Buddhism, Sikhism, and so on. I think these home-grown traditions have a very special, close relationship.

At the time of the Buddha, there were arguments or debates between Buddhist and non-

Buddhist traditions. Nagarjuna, Aryadeva, Buddhapalita, Chandrakirti, Dharmakirti, and, later, Shantarakshita and Kamalashila, and other great Buddhist masters wrote comprehensively about the ancient Hindu school of thought. This type of argument, I feel, is extremely useful and beautiful. Also, within Buddhism, there is a lot of argument, a lot of debate. I feel having two contradictory views and then arguing the merits of each is very helpful to sharpen the mind. These arguments are not like political fighting. These are very positive. I do feel that without them, Buddhist logic or thinking may become less developed. I feel these arguments and debates are very helpful, but people who are shortsighted or narrow-minded sometimes take a wrong view of these debates. The arguments then create divisions and lead to fighting and conflict. Therefore, I think it is worthwhile to welcome opposing views and to learn from them.

Buddha, during the early period of his life as a siddha, learned from the Hindu tradition. Then he experimented and later attained enlightenment. In doing this, he rejected many old Hindu traditions, ideas, and views but, simultaneously, accepted many of them, like shila, samadhi, and Vipassana. The demarcation between Buddhism and non-Buddhism is the theory of anatma and atma. I express anatma as my business: atma is their business. No problem!

I believe in anatma and, through this, I gain a lot of benefit. It helps my view and feelings. But to them, the atma theory or concept is very useful. I accept divisions like that. I feel that while I am trying to have closer relations with other traditions, I must make a greater effort to develop a better understanding of the views within those traditions.

So these are the main reasons why I attended the Kumbha Mela. After two days there, I was really satisfied. I admire the Hindu religious leaders who were there. They have very open minds. When I entered the meeting place, one leader firmly held my hand and recited the Buddhist prayer *Buddham Sharnam Gacchami*—beautiful, isn't it? Very beautiful. In his comments, he made it clear that Buddha promoted compassion, mahakaruna, and nonviolence. Later, another shankaracharya said that it is very important that we come closer. So that is wonderful. I feel this could be a new beginning.

An understandable but a sad thing is that some Buddhists in this country, especially neo-Buddhists, have a rather negative attitude toward Hindus. It's no use! Harboring negative feelings toward others is not the Buddhist way. On the Hindu side, I think the time has come to change the caste system and other outdated customs. We should openly state it: these customs are out of date. I wish for more concerted action to eliminate all negative feelings and negative things. If, instead of criticizing others, we try to understand them and improve our relations, politicians and other mischievous people who manipulate religious differences will eventually be isolated.

I really felt my pilgrimage to the Kumbha Mela was a good opportunity to make a little contribution. So, that's the story. Another important thing: before I reached there, I heard that there was a lot of dust. I expected that I might get flu. Fortunately, no flu in spite of the dust! Another thing that I want to share with our Buddhist friends, particularly the Tibetan Buddhists. More than twenty-five million human beings gathered at the Kumbha Mela, and the entire population was purely vegetarian. Not a single animal was sacrificed, and I think that is wonderful. If ten thousand Tibetans gathered, I think the butchers would be very busy. A bit unfortunate.

For a number of years, we and some monastic institutions have been making efforts to promote vegetarianism in monasteries. We must also make the effort when we have big gatherings. I think we should keep this in our mind.

To go back to the topic of emotions, without them, our lives will become colorless. Emotion can be very good, but I think the vital thing is that you have to make a distinction among the emotions. Some, in the short term, look colorful, but in the long run are destructive. Some are a little uncomfortable initially, but in the long run, there is an immense benefit. It is important to know and to be able to distinguish what kind of emotions are useful and which are negative and should be discarded. Here, firstly, all living beings, including plants, have the right to survive. Then, within the living beings, all those who have experiences of pain and pleasure have the right not only to survive but also to survive happily. That's our basic right. Sentient beings, or living beings who have the capacity to feel, who have cognition, have the desire to overcome suffering and pain, and achieve happiness and pleasure. There are two levels of experiences that bring pleasure or pain. One is mainly sensory. While seeing something good or beautiful, we can derive mental satisfaction. A beautiful sound can make us feel happy. In this regard, human beings and animals have similar experiences.

On the sensory level, we can experience satisfaction or joy or physical pain.

To human beings, the sensory level is very important. Therefore, material comforts and facilities are necessary and useful because they give us pleasure at this level. This would include a beautiful garden with birds and animals, the sound of music, good smells, fine taste, and also touch, including sexual experiences. We have these things in common with animals.

However, if we just focus on that level, we are not complete as human beings. Because of our intelligence, we have a better memory than animals, a greater ability to visualize and to see the long-range view—not just in our lifetimes but through many lifetimes and generations. Human beings have the capacity to retain memories of the long past: we have written and recorded thousands of years of experiences. But because of our intelligence, our sources of worry tend to increase. Because of this, sometimes, we have too many expectations and these bring in their wake doubt, fear, and suspicion. These are much stronger in us than in animals.

Obviously, some unhappy feelings result from human intelligence. This sort of unhappiness cannot be overcome by material comfort. We see rich people who have every material comfort and no need to worry but who are, nevertheless, mentally unhappy. So mental discomfort or dissatisfaction or restlessness cannot be removed by mere physical comfort. On the other hand, if on a mental level, there is happiness and satisfaction, physical discomfort can be easily handled. In some cases, undergoing physical difficulties can bring more mental satisfaction.

When you are mentally prepared, you are ready to face any amount of physical discomfort. So the mental level of experience is superior to the sensory level. That is why material progress or development is essential, but material gain alone cannot satisfy, cannot fulfill all human requirements. We human beings need more. The destroyer of our mental peace and comfort is that part of emotion that we call negative emotion.

Emotions like strong compassion, a sense of caring and concern for others, can be strongly felt, but they bring little disturbance to your mind. Actually, these emotions are deliberately developed and arise through training, through reasoning. They do not come instantly. But other emotions, such as anger and jealousy, come instantly, even though you may have some superficial reason for their appearance. And these emotions are usually destructive, whereas emotions such as strong karuna, compassion, and a sense of caring are, in the long run, beneficial, useful, and helpful. The distinction between negative and positive emotions is based on the fact that by nature we all want happiness and do not want suffering. Therefore, anything—external as well as internal—which ultimately brings happiness is positive. Anything which brings about a painful experience is negative. As far as the Buddhist thinking is concerned, the basic law is: we want happiness. Our basic right is to achieve happiness. So those things that produce deep satisfaction, joyfulness, and happiness are positive because this is what we seek. Negative emotions destroy our happiness.

I want to share with you three levels on which to counteract negative emotions. The first level follows secular ethics and does not touch any religious belief. It is to try to use our intelligence to analyze what happens in a given situation. We begin by identifying the long-term and short-term benefits or consequences of our negative emotions. When we become aware of their long-term negative consequences, we will deliberately restrain our negative emotions. Look at the possible consequences of a strong ill-will toward others, like hatred. As soon as a strong ill-will toward another develops, one's peace of mind immediately vanishes. And peaceful sleep also disappears. Eventually our digestion suffers. And, in this way, one's physical health is ruined. Strong negative emotions are destructive to peace of mind and good health. Also, if you have strong negative feelings toward others, eventually you feel that other people also have a similar kind of attitude. As a result, when you meet someone, feelings of suspicion, nervousness, and discomfort arise.

This kind of suspicious attitude is, I feel, against human nature because we are social animals. Whether we like it or not, we have to live in the human community; we can't survive in isolation. We put ourselves in a difficult situation when we deal negatively with those people upon whom we are dependent. I think the population of big cities looks like a human community, yet many individuals feel very lonely. Sometimes people do not trust and respect others.

Within any population, several people may be mischievous but, generally, if you treat people as brothers or sisters, they respond accordingly. We know, we can tell, that other people experience the same things we experience. I have anger and, similarly, others have anger. I sometimes have some jealousy, and others also have the same. There are no differences among us, so I treat others just like myself. Nothing to hide . . . open, straight. In this way, I think trust and friendship can develop.

You can clearly see that much of the unhappiness that we experience in life is due to errors of human intelligence: we don't analyze situations correctly so we experience negative emotions. To overcome negative emotions, we have to become aware of their long-term and short-term consequences. We also have to analyze the reality of the situation. Reality is made of interdependent parts. Things happen because of many causes and conditions. That is reality. But in our mind, in our perception, if some unhappy things happen, we point to one cause and blame it. Then we develop anger. But if we think more carefully, if we are realistic in our assessment, we know these things happen because of many causes and conditions, which include one's mental attitude. Therefore, if we know that in reality, there are many causes, we won't blame a single factor.

Similarly, good things happen because of many causes, many factors. If we understand this, there is not much of a basis for making a distinction between good and bad. If someone takes advantage of us, it is wrong, it is unjust, we have to stop that. We have to take countermeasures but without negative emotions. That is possible and actually such measures are more effective. So through an awareness of reality and the resultant consequences, we can change our attitude. Eventually, we can develop a clear conviction that certain emotions are useless and may prove harmful. Once we develop this conviction, our attitude toward negative emotions is more distanced; we do not welcome them. But until we develop this belief, we will mistake these negative, destructive emotions as part of our mind, as part of us.

In this connection, I am not talking of religious matters, but simply out of a sense of caring for one another, looking at others as a part of my community. Actually, we are all part of the community of humanity. If humanity is happy, has a successful life, a happy future, automatically, I will benefit. If humanity suffers, I too will suffer. Humanity is like one body, and we are part of that body. Once you realize this, once you cultivate this kind of attitude, you can bring about a change in your way of thinking. A sense of caring, commitment, discipline, oneness with humanity—these are very relevant in today's world. I call this secular ethics, and this is the first level to counter negative emotions.

The second level in this connection is taught by all major religious traditions, whether Christian or

Muslim or Jewish or Hindu. They all carry the message of love, compassion, forgiveness, tolerance, contentment, and discipline. These are countermeasures for negative emotions. When anger is about to surface, when hatred is about to flare up, think of tolerance. It is important to stop any mental dissatisfaction when we feel it because it leads to anger and hatred.

Patience is the countermeasure for mental dissatisfaction. Greed and its self-centeredness—I want this, I want that—brings unhappiness and also destruction of the environment, exploitation of others, and increases the gap between the rich and the poor. The countermeasure is contentment. When you are greedy, if you experience even a little jolt in your happiness, you will be totally disrupted. So practicing contentment is useful in our daily lives. Self-discipline is resisting giving in to negative emotions and is a way to protect oneself from long-term disaster. This discipline does not refer to an order but is undertaken to save oneself from a long-term miserable life.

All religious traditions talk about methods of compassion and forgiveness. If we accept religion, we should take the religious methods seriously and sincerely and use them in our daily lives. Then, a meaningful life can develop. Otherwise, nothing changes. For example, we Tibetans can carry a rosary and recite something, but our minds can be somewhere else. Some of our Christian brothers and sisters can go to church on Sunday and perhaps for a short moment close their eyes, but then they might resume a life where nothing has changed. The real practice is outside, not inside the church, because we encounter our real-life situations outside the church where we face every possibility for anger, jealousy, attachment, and so forth. Therefore, the real practice is to be done outside our places of worship.

Recently, I met a Christian minister who asked for my opinion. He felt that people were not interested in Christian doctrines because they felt it had little relevance to our daily life. In my opinion, this is not due to any shortcoming of the Christian message, but due to a wrong emphasis. Religious practice is not just prayer but is using the methods I mentioned before: love, compassion, forgiveness. If these methods are taken seriously and put into practice in one's daily life, they are relevant. For example, if you are about to lose your temper, remember, if you practice tolerance, God will be happy. If you see good things, greed and attachment develop. Then you remember you are a follower of God and are supposed to fulfill the wishes of God. Contentment follows, and greed disappears. If we sincerely apply the essence of any major religious tradition, it automatically has relevance to our daily lives. Life becomes more meaningful. This is the second level of countermeasures to overcome negative emotions.

The third level is the Buddhist way. Basically, if you try to trace the roots of all types of afflictive emotions like anger and so forth, you will find four misconceptions. One is the misconception about different types of realities. For example, we tend to see what is impermanent as permanent and everlasting. That leads to suffering and mental disturbance. Similarly, we tend to see suffering as happiness. For example, we see contaminated experiences as a source of pleasure and happiness. And, similarly, we tend to see what is impure as pure. We are unable to see the impurity of our psychophysical body and tend to regard it as something clean and pure and get attached to it. Also, we are inclined to see what is selfless as having some existential self, an independent self. Basically, these kinds of misconceptions aggravate our minds and from them we develop different types of afflictive emotions.

Because of this, the Buddha taught the thirty-seven limbs to enlightenment to counter these misconceptions. In these, he spoke about maintaining the four mindfulnesses. The first mindfulness addresses the misconception regarding the nature of your body. The actual nature of your body is such that it is made up of different types of unclean substances. When you study and reflect closely on it, you are able to see that the body has an impure nature, an impermanent nature. Whether you examine the nature of your body in terms of its cause or its present entity, you will find that it is impure, unclean. For example, if you reflect on the cause of the physical body, the cause is the amalgamation of the semen and the ovum that come from your parents.

In terms of its present entity and nature, you can examine your body right from the top of your head to the soles of your feet, and you will find that it is impure and unclean in nature. If you look at what is produced by the body—urine, excretion, and so forth—you will see only unclean substances. So, in fact, the body is like a machine that produces these unclean substances. When this machine runs well, the shape or color of things coming from it are quite good, but if something is wrong, a lot of unusual things happen. Actually, the most expensive and beautiful things consumed are made dirty by this machine. Think along these lines.

Not only that, but the body also acts as the basis for further suffering. You will find that the psychophysical body is made of a combination and coexistence of four basic elements. When you see the nature of these four elements—fire, water, earth, and air—you realize that they are conflicting in nature. When we say, "I am happy" or "I am healthy," we are saying we are healthy in the sense that these conflicting four elements are equal in their power. When there is a slight change in the balance of power of these elements, you get some disease. The ease is out of balance.

I am more than sixty-six years old. Until now, this body has survived because of many reasons. But for the body merely to survive . . . what meaning does this have? However, if our marvelous human intelligence survives and functions normally, we can try to cultivate infinite altruism and a deeper understanding of reality. That is wonderful: that is the Buddhist viewpoint. So think along these lines. In this way, if you reflect properly, you will be able to understand clearly how we perceive this impure body as something pure and clean.

When we talk about the second misconception, that of perceiving what is suffering as happiness, we are not talking on a gross, ordinary level because at a superficial, ordinary level, nobody identifies suffering as happiness. We are talking on a more profound level. As I mentioned earlier, there are two types of feelings: feelings at the level of the body and those at the level of the mind. Most physical happiness arises due to a decrease of physical unhappiness. For example, if you have been shivering in the cold for some time and have suddenly run to the sunlight and stay there, you feel satisfied and happy. There is no particular satisfaction in that sunlight: it only brings a decrease of suffering from cold.

To prove this point, if it were a long-lasting, genuine happiness, something independent, you should be able to stay in that sunlight for a long time and your happiness should increase rather than decrease. But that is not the case. After a while, you will feel hot, and will need to move into the shade again. The original feeling of happiness and satisfaction will change into suffering if you stay in the sunlight for too long. In many cases, a pleasurable physical feeling seems good, satisfactory, and enjoyable, but on a closer analysis, if continued, it becomes uncomfortable.

Regarding the mental feeling of happiness, as long as you are under the control of afflictive emotions, the mind is not independent, it is not free. Therefore, if you reflect properly, you will clearly

understand that your mind will definitely encounter suffering even if you feel temporarily
happy. For example, if you are suffering from a
chronic disease, you may not encounter acute pain
every moment, but you are not healthy; you are
not free from that chronic disease.

The third misconception is that of seeing what
is impermanent as permanent. It is because of a
strong grasping at the self that, in our daily life, we
tend to see our experience of happiness as something that is going to last for a long time, something that is going to last forever. We tend to
perceive these things as permanent. For example,
when I am passing through an old castle, I think
that at the time the castle was built, the king felt,
naturally, that it was permanent. Look at the Great
Wall of China. Throughout many years, so many
people, through great hardships, built that wall.
The emperor thought that his kingdom was a permanent one. Now, there is nothing left except parts
of the wall. Look at Hitler, Stalin, Mao Tse-tung.
Each had very strong feelings of "my" region,
"my" ideology, "my" power, and they mercilessly
killed millions of people to try to make these things
permanent.

It is useful to reflect on impermanence. Of this,
there are two levels. One is very subtle. The other

is the impermanence of continuity, like the death of a plant, the cessation of any life. We can actually see the end of continuity. This is possible because things are changing from moment to moment. If things are not changing, observing the end of continuity is impossible. The coming to an end of any solid object in terms of its continuity is possible because there is a constant change taking place in all impermanent phenomena. By observing and perceiving the disintegration of the continuity of an object or impermanent phenomenon, we can conclude the changing nature of all types of impermanent phenomena.

To understand the nature of impermanence and disintegration, we should realize that every impermanent phenomenon, at the moment that it comes into existence, does so in the nature of change, in the nature of disintegration. This is more useful than trying to understand it in the sense that something has finally disintegrated and is no more.

The fourth misconception is to regard what is selfless as having a self and as having an independent existence. Regarding the interpretation of the meaning of selflessness, there are various Buddhist philosophical schools giving different interpretations and explanations. The common Buddhist understanding of the meaning of selflessness is that there is no self which is self-sufficient, self-supporting, and inherently existing. Once we are able to understand that there is no self which is self-supporting and self-sufficient, we will be able to counter the misconception that there is such a self. Once we are able to realize this misconception, we will be able to reduce grasping, attachment, and anger. The stronger your sense of self as being self-supporting and self-sufficient, the greater will be your attachment toward your body, your house, your relatives, and so forth. On the other hand, the greater your understanding of the absence of such a self, the less will be your attachment toward material objects.

The Buddha taught not only the selflessness of the person, but also the selflessness of all phenomena. This means that not only does a person lack a self-supporting and self-sufficient existence, but also the objects enjoyed by that person merely have the appearance of a permanent existence. We tend to see the external, material objects that we enjoy as having an independent, inherent existence, but there are no such objects and no such enjoyment.

With regard to the explanation of how things do not exist as they appear to us, there are, again, different philosophical interpretations. According to the Mind-Only (Cittamatra) school of thought, though things appear to us as having an external existence, in reality, there is no such external existence. Everything is in the nature of the mind. Then, according to the Madhyamika or Middle Way school of thought, things do not exist in the way they appear to us. If you analyze carefully, you find that all perceived things do not have an independent or inherent existence but are rather like an illusion. They are conditioned by our sensory faculties and the mind.

The more profound your understanding of the selflessness of the person and the selflessness of the thought, the more you will be able to understand the other side of the coin—the interconnectedness of everything. Even though things do not have an independent existence, they are closely interdependent and interconnected.

So, in our understanding of the four misconceptions, the first three understandings are antidotes that would repudiate their misconceptions. By understanding the fourth misconception, we would uproot the seed of the misconception of the self.

Thus, there are different ways to combat negative emotions: the Hinayana way, the Bodhisattva way, and the Tantrayana way. While there are differences among the three, they all have the same aim: the complete elimination of negative emotions. That is nirvana.

In practice, people often want a concrete method to overcome these mental discomforts. However, it is impossible to practice one method and immediately relieve all anxieties. I think it is like the health of the body. When our body, constitution, and immune system are healthy, we can immediately counteract and remove an infection. But if the body's basic immune system is weak, even a slight infection is very difficult to remove. Similarly, if your basic mental attitude is healthy and strong through training, knowledge, and conviction, and something tragic happens—if you lose your parent or a person dear to you, or if an injustice occurs, or if you develop an incurable illness—your healthy mental attitude will be sufficient to counter it. You can maintain your peace of mind and can handle any unfortunate thing more peacefully, more positively.

If your mental attitude has not had sufficient training, overcoming problems will be difficult. Training the mind is very essential. To train properly, you must have conviction, which comes only if you analyze thoroughly. In order to do this, you need a lot of material and a lot of information. So, you see, the Buddhist way of practice begins with study. Study by hearing, by reading, just absorbing information! Once you gather the information, you have to analyze it yourself. Don't just rely on Buddha's quotations. Rely instead on your investigations and experiments. This is the way you can develop a firm conviction, which, eventually, makes the difference in your mental attitude.

Hence, in order to overcome our negative emotions, we need to use our intelligence to analyze. We must also develop, with the help of intelligence, positive emotions like strong faith and compassion. In this way, wisdom and positive emotions can grow side by side. Proper faith and compassion must be based on reason and intelligence: that is the Buddhist way. And that is the way to overcome negative emotions, to finish them, to stop them.

Your Holiness, at the Kumbha Mela, did you go for a dip in the Ganges?

No, I didn't, but I put a few drops of water here. That is sufficient.

Your Holiness, please give your views about God and lives before and after death.

What is God? The word God, in one sense, means infinite love. I think Buddhists accept that. But Buddhists do not accept God in the sense of something supreme, in the center, or something absolute, a creator. Buddhists find a lot of contradictions regarding that concept. I think Christians, along with the notion of a creator, accept just one life, this very life, created by God. I think that idea is very powerful, has its own beauty. And that concept, you see, creates a feeling of intimacy with God.

Once we dislike a person, why do we continue to do so? It is very difficult to change our attitude.

I think this is because you are just focusing on anger. Everything is relative. If you look at the same object from different angles, you can see differently. For example, we lost our country, and our country has experienced a lot of destruction. If we think only from that angle, there is great disturbance and sadness. But because of this tragedy, we became refugees and have had many occasions to interact with different people—religious people, scientists, ordinary people—and that is very useful and a good opportunity to learn. If one thinks along these lines, the same tragic situation has, on the one side, very sad implications and, on the other, new opportunities. It is useful to try to see issues from different angles. And it also helps to make comparisons. When tragic things happen, you can think what it would be like if worse things had happened. When you make a comparison, you see that your situation is far better. The way you perceive a situation, even though it remains the same, makes a big difference to your mental attitude.

What should be the spiritual limit of ambition for a busy professional?

As I mentioned earlier, while you are conducting business, you have the opportunity to practice self-discipline, contentment, tolerance, and patience. But to do that, first you have to study, you have to develop the conviction that some emotions are destructive while others are useful. Once you develop this distinction clearly, this awareness about what is useful and what is harmful, this practice can be carried over to your daily life. Spiritual practice does not mean that you just remain seated in meditation, doing nothing.

That is not necessarily spiritual practice. Pigeons, when their stomachs are full with food, also meditate. They are very godlike, perfectly still. So that is nothing, no help. In one sense, meditation means to withdraw all our senses and remain in thoughtlessness. But by itself, that is nothing and has little effect. However, there are some practices, some meditations, which need thoughtlessness as a basis. Then, within the thoughtlessness, some other, deeper wisdom develops: that is something different. But otherwise, just mere thoughtlessness is nothing.

If this body is the basis of suffering and is impure, why is it believed to be the only vehicle to salvation?

This is primarily explained in terms of the wonderful human intelligence and the clear light, too. There is not much difference between animals and human beings. But at this moment, we have no possibility to utilize that subtle mind. In order to do so, we have to use the normal human intelligence. So, on a grosser level of mind, there is intelligence, and the brain makes the difference. Human brains have the capacity to have a sophisticated intelligence. Using the grosser level of human intelligence and trying to utilize the subtle mind is impossible for animals. Although, when they die, they have the same experiences, yet it is impossible for them to employ the subtle mind. Judging from that, the human body is a precious thing, but not in the sense that it is something good itself.

Your Holiness, could you throw some more light on the distinction between narrow-mindedness and broad-mindedness?

If we think just about today, that is narrow-mindedness, and if we disregard today's experiences and think about the future, it is broad-mindedness. Thinking only for oneself is narrow-mindedness, but the awareness that my future is related to the future of others, that my interests entirely depend on the interests of the others and if I take care about their interests, my interests automatically are fulfilled—I think this is a more broad-minded outlook. So, in taking care of your neighbor, ultimately, you will benefit. If you don't care for your neighbor, ultimately you will suffer . . . like that!

Does selflessness also mean forgetting oneself, for the sake of others?

That is not the meaning. For example, when we talk about the development of altruism, or the wish to achieve enlightenment for the sake of all sentient beings, even though the altruism is primarily targeted toward benefiting other sentient beings, you simultaneously aspire to achieve enlightenment, or the state of Buddhahood, for yourself. While thinking about yourself, if you totally ignore other sentient beings and disregard them, that is wrong. But, on the other hand, if you faithfully and sensibly help other sentient beings, your own purpose is also fulfilled. It is because of this that even when we think of the ultimate achievement in the form of Buddhahood, we talk about the rupakaya and the dharmakaya, or the form body and the truth body, and we normally designate two different terms to these two bodies. We talk about dharmakaya as the body for oneself, and the rupakaya as the body for others. So even though you think about others and work for them, your purpose is fulfilled, as a by-product, so to say.

Are there different kinds of negative emotions?

There are eighty-four thousand types of afflictive emotions that have been explained in the text. Even though a fixed number has been given in the text, the different types of negative emotions that can arise in our minds is definitely limitless. And in the

Abhidharma, a clear identification of what is known as the six root afflictive emotions and twenty secondary afflictive emotions has been made.

To what extent can one sacrifice in real-life situations?

In the teaching of the Buddha, unless you reach a certain required level of realization, sacrificing your body for others is actually discouraged. So you have to calculate in terms of the long-term benefit, the short-time benefit, and so forth. If you have a strong conviction and confidence because of your high realization, sacrificing one's body for the benefit of other sentient beings is encouraged and recommended.

Does the soul come with its complete destiny or is there free will?

According to Buddhism, there is free will. Even when we talk about different types of karma, about having to experience their consequences and about those so-called definitive karmas whose results are to be experienced in this life . . . even in such cases, it is in the sense that if you do not provide or develop any positive counterforces to react against negative karmas, you are bound to experience those results. But if you make an effort and develop certain positive counterforces, even the so-called definitive karma can be changed. So much depends on how you think and what kind of karma you accumulate. In fact, karma is collected by the person, the individual, and I think this happens according to free will.

Who was greater: Lord Buddha or Siddhartha, who sacrificed his life to become the Buddha?

In one of the sutras, it is explained that if a bodhisattva is coming in a chariot, if nobody is pulling the chariot, and an enlightened buddha sees that, he should go and pull the chariot in which the bodhisattva is sitting. I think that is great. Buddhas have all the fulfilment, power, and omniscience. Buddhas have already reached the highest state of enlightenment and power in terms of spiritual development. In the case of bodhisattvas—whether the bodhisattva is in the category of those who have not eliminated the obscurations to enlightenment and nirvana, or is among those bodhisattvas who have not completely removed the afflictive emotions—are still under obscurations and under the bondage of afflictive emotions, they are still completely dedicated to the welfare of other sentient beings. This is really inspiring, and such bodhisattvas are objects of appreciation and admiration. Of course, this is dependent on your perspective at these two different things.

If you look at the buddha, a totally enlightened being, from the perspective of his omniscience, the buddha is greater. If you perceive the bodhisattva from the perspective of how much he sacrifices himself for the benefit of other sentient beings, even though he is not enlightened, you can see the greatness of the bodhisattva.

How do you stay positive when you get overwhelmed by environmental and human injustice?

For a beginner, being confronted with such problems is a difficult task, an uphill task. Here you need more training, practice, and understanding. So for those practitioners who are at the initial stage, it is important to remain more isolated and to make some kind of a preparation. Once you have gained inner strength and self-confidence, then the world, the external environment, can become your practice. The more disturbed the area is, the more your practice can develop and progress.

What comfort can Buddhism offer to people in times of great suffering, like this earthquake?

That depends a lot on the person's belief or faith. It hinges on whom you approach.

For a Buddhist, such events can generate thinking about the suffering nature of samsara and impermanence. If you have the proper motivation, a tragic and painful experience can be useful in reducing your wrong concepts. It can explain such points as the infallible law of cause and effect and also how through experiencing such problems, in the long run, you can purify yourself from certain negative consequences.

However, the humane way is to go there and share the suffering of those who have been affected and show sympathy and concern. That itself makes a difference. I think by doing that, we can relieve their suffering. Also, of course, medical help, donations, and other practical means should be used to help them.

Your Holiness, can you tell us a little bit about dakinis?

Dakini . . . I don't know. I think, dakinis exist on a mysterious level. Sometimes it is possible to communicate with certain dakinis. Then, we believe that among women we find them in human form. How does one investigate? That is difficult! In fact, I believe that among sadhus at the Kumbha Mela, there could be some practitioners with great experience. For example, there are those who are completely naked, and—I was told—remained in the mountains for the entire year, for many years. They must have some sort of experience, otherwise it would be impossible for them to remain there. Actually, before I went there, I asked if it was possible to see some of these sadhus. But that is difficult unless there is some individual who knows a particular sadhu and introduces you. Otherwise, you just meet some naked sadhu, and you take a photograph and otherwise nothing . . . useless.

In ancient times, Tilopa, Naropa, Gompopa, all of whom were great siddhas, looked just like beggars. While some were hunters, others were fishermen and some were just beggars. Only if we were to spend months with them and investigate their daily lives, behavior, expressions, could we come to know their inner experiences. Generally, those people who have deep inner experiences don't show them on the outside. Then, those people who have not much inside, they often show something outside . . . something big, something big, isn't it?

If God created the universe, who created God?

That is the Buddhist question. So, that is why we do not accept God.

What is the best way to teach compassion?

I have reservations about the best, the quickest, the easiest, the cheapest. . . .

Now many more new translations of Buddhist texts are coming out, and good books concerning Buddhism are already available. Read these books, study, and you will find the answer. Then you choose the best one!

Is it possible for an ordinary man to attain enlightenment playing all the games of the universe?

Generally speaking, yes, in the long run, it is possible. There is a beautiful verse by Phabongkha Rinpoche, which reads something like this: If you practice sincerely, even if you remain a householder, you will attain enlightenment as had happened in the case of Marpa and Milarepa and many other Indian and Tibetan kings and ministers. If you do not practice, even if you stay in the mountains for a long time, you will only be like the marmot hibernating for several months in the ground of the mountains.

What was the most difficult situation for Your Holiness to overcome?

I don't know. I think that is difficult to say. I think depending on certain times on certain levels. For example, around my thirties, I had some understanding about sunya (wisdom), and then I developed the sense of a possibility to achieve nirvana. Therefore, the renunciation became, I think, fairly strong, but then at that time, I found it very difficult to think about bodhicitta.

In my forties, I studied Shantideva's book, also Nagarjuna's *Precious Garland,* and some other books, and I thought more about bodhicitta. Of course, I still have no genuine experience of bodhicitta or shunya, but, comparatively, sometimes now I have the feeling and confidence that if I have sufficient time, I can develop proper bodhicitta as well as shunyata. At a different time, according to the experiences of that time, I thought this is very difficult. After some time, I feel this is not so difficult. So, I don't know, there are many difficulties, and then at the same time, as I mentioned before, there are possibilities to overcome all these obstacles. Then, as Dalai Lama, there is the difficulty of Tibet's situation. That is very difficult; it is actually beyond my control, isn't it? Very difficult.

In conclusion, those people who believe in spiritual value, especially Buddha Dharma, should study! Implement these values in your daily life. And try to be a good follower of Buddha Dharma and of Buddha Sakyamuni, our teacher. We should be good students: that is important. You see, whether one is a believer or a nonbeliever, whether there is a reason or not, we are born on this earth. So, as long as we remain on this planet, be a sensible person, a warmhearted person. If we can be useful to others, be like that; if not, there is no reason to create more trouble for others!

Sir Shankerlal Hall, Modern School, 2001

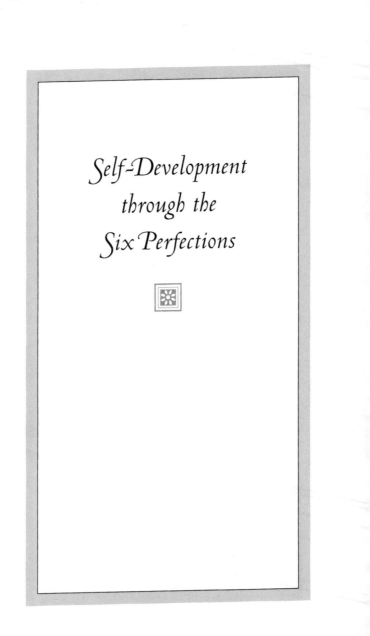

Self-Development
through the
Six Perfections

When people come to listen to me, many do so with the intention to get a message or a technique for securing inner peace and for achieving a successful life.

Some people may have come simply out of curiosity, but the important thing is that we should know we are all the same, all human beings. I am nothing special: I am just a simple Buddhist monk. Just one human being. And we all have the potential for good as well as for bad. Also, we all have the right to lead happy lives. This means happy days and nights; in this way, our lives become happy.

I would like to explain some essential things. As you know, the main distinction between human beings and nonhuman beings or other mammals is, I think, human intelligence. Feelings of pain and happiness, the desire for peace and pleasure, and the wish to overcome pain are common in human beings and in animals. Even insects . . . small insects have the same desires. But we human beings have intelligence. We also have a greater power of memory and vision about things. So we have, like other mammals or animals, physical experiences of good or bad, but we have additional feelings because of our intelligence. Our memories, visions, and expectations for the distant future sometimes cause us anxiety and fear, doubt and worry, even when things are okay.

Because of our ability to envision a distant future, not only for ourselves and our generation, but also for our children and for our children's children, for future generations and future centuries, our mental suffering and worries are proportionately more. Since we have greater intelligence and thinking power than other mammals, we are susceptible to more experiences of mental sufferings than them. Since mental sufferings and anxieties are a product of intelligence, the only way to solve them is through using our intelligence. There is no other way. Even people who have enormous material resources at their disposal have problems and sufferings. This clearly indicates that mental sufferings that are the products of intelligence cannot be solved by material facilities.

There is another important factor. I feel that mental experiences are superior to physical experiences. If someone has physical problems due to sickness or poverty, but if that person is mentally happy, the suffering caused by physical problems can be subdued and will not be too disturbing. On the other hand, if someone is mentally disturbed, even great physical comfort will not weaken or alleviate the mental suffering or turmoil. While we make every effort to ensure material development, it is important to look inward. We must not neglect our inner values.

Today, in many parts of our world, we are facing a crisis of morality. In science and technology, there is no basis on which to demarcate between moral and immoral. What is material is just material, and money is just money. There is no basis for wrong and right unless one makes a connection with the inner experiences of sentient beings. The basis for judging what is right or wrong is the degree of satisfaction or pain it brings to sentient beings. If something brings satisfaction, we usually call it right because we all want happiness and satisfaction. As we do not want suffering or pain, all the things that make us uncomfortable or which bring suffering are considered bad by us. So when we talk about right or wrong, the demarcation has to be made in connection with internal human feelings. Apart from them, we cannot talk about right or wrong in connection with external material things. In today's world, we often give importance only to material things. From that point of view, as long as one gains more money or power, everything is justified. Other issues are not considered, and everything is based on satisfying greed.

The recent events in New York on September 11, 2001, were, of course, tragic. A group of people used their intelligence to plan these events if not for years at least for a few months. They used airplanes full of fuel as explosives and also full of passengers. So there was not only sophisticated intelligence but also strong hatred. The point is that human intelligence, the sophisticated human mind, guided or controlled by any negative emotion is a real disaster. Unless we have a sense of moral conduct, human beings are bound to face problems and difficulties. Therefore, when we talk about observing certain moral disciplines, we must also talk about guiding emotions.

Recently, I was in Baroda in one of the institutions of Swami Narayan. There I observed that monks staying in that monastery observe a pure moral conduct, vows and disciplines, and also help in improving the condition of society. This kind of institution can be found in other places as well. It is extremely important that energy from these different institutions and organizations and from individuals should be brought together. Bringing together positive energies is extremely important. Bishop Tutu has said that different religious institutions and organizations should participate in those areas where people are confronting different types of problems. Not only will their problems be addressed but the common effort will also bring different religions closer. We must try to promote harmony among various religious traditions. It is important for followers of each tradition to practice sincerely and seriously. Suppose we are Buddhists. In order to promote human values, we must, first, make every effort to improve ourselves. In that way, we will prove to be a good example to others. Instead of thinking of conversion, we would think about how much we can contribute through our tradition.

We are all part of humanity, and each of us has the responsibility to improve humanity and to bring it additional happiness in order to make it more peaceful, friendlier, and compassionate. So, if one individual practices compassion and forgiveness sincerely and regularly, wherever he or she may live, it will generate a positive atmosphere. That is a way to contribute toward the betterment of humanity. Also, through practicing one's tradition, a person eventually has inner spiritual experiences. This enables that person to see the value of other traditions. Therefore, to promote religious harmony, one should look into one's tradition seriously and implement it as much as one can.

In order to develop seriousness about your faith or tradition, you must find something relevant to your everyday life. If you follow your tradition merely as a habit or custom, it will not have much of an impact in transforming your mind. For example, some Tibetans, Ladakhis, and Chinese who have been practicing Buddhism from the time of their forefathers take it for granted that Buddhism is a part of their tradition and culture. They do not develop a sincerity about the message inherent in the Buddha's teaching. On the other hand, when some people who have not been born and brought up as Buddhists first take an interest in Buddhism, they internalize the Buddha's teaching with great enthusiasm and appreciation. You can see their sincerity. So it is vital to study with seriousness. This is especially true of the Buddha Dharma because in order to transform our emotions, we have to employ our intelligence in the maximum way possible. To develop spiritual faith, we must use our intelligence. I think that is unique to Buddhism. That is why the writings of the Nalanda Masters are full of reasoning, logic, arguments, the raising of different sorts of doubts, and then explanations, comparisons, and analyses.

Thus, the Buddhist way to transform our emotions works not through faith or prayer but through the maximum use of intelligence and reasoning. As you know, there are three levels to this. On one level, it is difficult to use our reasoning, and we have to rely on someone else's word. But here, too, we have to investigate whether that other person—including the Buddha himself—is reliable or not. Therefore, for the Buddhist practitioner study is very essential.

In the arrangement of the thangkas here, the Buddha is placed in the northernmost direction with the master next to him. It looks like he is debating with the Buddha! The Buddha gave us the liberty to question his words. Questions are very important. Without questions, we cannot get a proper answer. Without skepticism, without doubt, without investigation, we have no satisfactory answers. Therefore, in the Buddhist tradition, intelligence is used to its maximum extent and study is essential.

I will now refer to personal development through the six perfections. When we talk about perfections, first of all, we have to establish the meaning of the word "perfection," which means "going beyond." "Beyond" here refers to the place or path of enlightenment. And that place or path is called "beyond" with reference to the place where we normally exist, in our ordinary form. In this context, when we talk about the Four Noble Truths, the first two truths, that is, true suffering and true origin of suffering, are on this ordinary side, and the other two truths, true path and true cessation, are the paths beyond. Here, when we use the word "beyond," we refer to true types of enlightenment. The word refers to having gone beyond the cycle of existence, the cycle of samsaric existence, and therefore when we talk about the word "beyond," it could refer to the total extinction of afflictive emotions and suffering and, thereby, the achievement of liberation. Also there is the greater form of enlightenment, which is the state of Buddhahood. Here, we are mainly talking about that meaning when we use the word "beyond."

The Tibetan word for enlightenment is *jangchub*, which means to internalize the necessary positive qualities in their totality. Therefore, the word "enlightenment" in this sense has two meanings: it can refer to the path that leads to the resultant state of Buddhahood, or it can refer to the resultant state of Buddhahood itself. So it refers both to the path and the fruit. Therefore, when we use the word "perfection" or "beyond," there are two viewpoints from different scholars.

According to one opinion, the word "perfection" can be used in connection with the path as well as with the fruit. The other opinion says that the word "perfection" can be used only in reference to the fruit and not to the path. Now, here if we use "perfection" in the sense of the path which leads to enlightenment, it is a kind of perfection which is followed on the stage of training. Even when we use "perfection" in reference to the path, we cannot talk about all kinds of paths as perfection paths. For example, in the case of the practice of giving or generosity, giving and generosity in general cannot be termed perfections. However, when giving and generosity are influenced by the practice of method, that is the development of bodhicitta. When influenced by wisdom-realizing emptiness, these practices, even if they are in the stage of learning, can be called perfections. In the case of giving or generosity, we have a practice that is found within the practices of a bodhisattva and also a practice that is followed by non-Buddhists, within non-Buddhist schools. For example, not to kill. When not killing is practiced from fear of the law, it has nothing to do with religious practice.

Every action is dependent on motivation, whether the action is virtuous or nonvirtuous, and for a virtuous action, whether it becomes a cause for liberation or not, or whether it becomes a cause for Buddhahood or not. Therefore, in order to make your practice one of perfection, you should have the clear goal of enlightenment, along with the wish that your enlightenment goes beyond liberation just for yourself.

When we aim to achieve the great enlightenment, or Buddhahood, the path that we need to cultivate is an altruistic one, based on the wish to achieve enlightenment for the sake of all sentient beings. The motivation involves many activities and deeds to benefit other sentient beings. Therefore, it is important to possess this special feature of the mind which intends to help all suffering beings in order to achieve enlightenment.

Another aspect of the great enlightenment or Buddhahood is that it is a state free from all elaborations. When we talk about such a state, we can have different meanings. It may mean that when you achieve the state of Buddhahood, it is devoid of various types of contaminations, pollutions, suffering, and afflictive emotions. Enlightenment of such a kind is not only free from these kinds of things but also from various dualistic appearances. When you achieve such a state, you are unfettered from all elaborations in the form of subject-object duality and appearances of conventionality.

You are free not because the subject-object duality or conventional appearances are objects of elimination in the sense that they are negative emotions. Rather, you are free because these elaborations cease to exist when you reach the state of enlightenment. In such a state, the mind of enlightenment or omniscience is such that it is totally merged with emptiness. To such a mind, no elaborations exist. When you reach that state of enlightenment, it has two aspects and features. One is that after having reached such a state of enlightenment, one has the capacity to spontaneously and effortlessly fulfill the wishes of sentient beings. That kind of possibility is a result of having developed the altruistic motivation to achieve enlightenment for the sake of all sentient beings when you are in the stage of training.

Another aspect of the state of enlightenment is that it is free from all types of elaborations, as we have explained, and the cause of achieving such a state is the development of wisdom-realizing emptiness. The omniscient state is a product of causes and factors. It is a conditioned phenomenon. Since the omniscient state is a product of causes and factors, it is within the purview of the law of causality. Therefore, this system of path and effect, path and fruit, is within the context of interdependent origination. The sufferings that we encounter arise from their respective causes and conditions. Similarly, the happinesses that we experience are dependent on their respective causes and conditions.

The highest form of happiness, in the form of enlightenment, also arises from causes and conditions. In this way, these things happen within the context of causality. Any type of result or fruit occurs by depending on those causes and conditions that have the capacity to produce that particular kind of result. It is because of this that in one of the sutras, the Buddha mentions that sweet products and fruits can be produced from sweet seeds. Similarly, sour products and fruits result from sour seeds. Therefore, the various sublime qualities that we see in the state of Buddhahood or enlightenment must come from the capacities and potential we have. In their absence, it is not possible to achieve a state of Buddhahood or to develop the qualities of the Buddha.

In the state of enlightenment, we have two bodies of the Buddha that are known as the form body and the truth body, rupakaya and dharmakaya. The form body of the Buddha is one which spontaneously and effortlessly appears before sentient beings to help them. The truth body, as we have discussed earlier, is a state free from all types of elaborations. The cause of achieving the form body is the development and practice of bodhicitta, and the cause of actualizing the truth body is the wisdom-realizing emptiness.

If we try to simplify the meaning of the wisdom-realizing emptiness and of bodhicitta, we can say that the wisdom-realizing emptiness is the best form of intelligence, the summit of its development, and that bodhicitta is the best form of human emotion. We realize that we already have the basis for both. We have emotions, the capacity to judge, and intelligence. Therefore, when we outline the teachings of the Buddha, we do so with three major points: We have the presentation of the foundational qualities which relate to the law of nature. We have the level of the path where we engage in those practices of the path which conform to the law of nature. And through these practices, we actualize a fruit in the form of enlightenment; this also conforms to the path. Thus, we use the word "perfection" in relation to those practices on the training stage influenced by bodhicitta and wisdom-realizing emptiness.

There could be two types of wisdom-realizing emptiness. The first refers to being unable to see emptiness directly but realizing emptiness through a kind of generic image. The second kind is perceived or discerned directly and does not depend on a medium or generic image. So when we talk about practices influenced by wisdom and method, it refers to those types of wisdom that directly discern emptiness. Likewise, when we talk about the need to develop bodhicitta, which is the mind that cherishes the welfare of other sentient beings, we see that it is possible to develop such a mind because within us we have this self-cherishing attitude. We are able to develop such an attitude because we have a feeling of closeness to ourselves. We have a kind of self-love and, based on this, we develop a self-cherishing attitude.

Similarly, if you develop a feeling of closeness to other people, other sentient beings, you can use that to develop a wish that cherishes the welfare of other people, of other sentient beings. So first there should be a kind of self-love, a cherishing mind toward oneself, because in the absence of being able to appreciate oneself, it is not possible, or it is difficult, to develop a mind cherishing the welfare of other sentient beings. Basically, we all have a feeling of closeness to ourselves. Even in cases of apparent self-hatred, some kind of self-cherishing attitude lies deep within us.

It is from cherishing oneself that one can gradually extend a similar attitude to others. Even animals have a limited altruism, particularly those whose offspring depend on them for a period. Naturally, there would be a bond of special love. So this love, this natural feeling of appreciation, comes from a biological need because the structure, the formation of the body, is such that you are compelled to depend on love. In order to survive, we need to care for one another. We already have the seed of love or compassion or affection for others because we have affection for ourselves. That is the seed.

The question arises, how to develop infinite altruism? It seems that it is possible to develop infinite altruism through wisdom and intelligence. Normally, when one talks about the need to cultivate love and compassion for others, one feels that this will be of benefit and help to others, but of no help to oneself, or irrelevant to oneself. This is a mistaken viewpoint because when you develop love and compassion for others, you are able to mentally develop profound satisfaction and courage. As a result you, the practitioner, benefit. You will have less fear, more willpower, more self-confidence. Automatically, one mentally becomes calmer. As to how much your expression of love and compassion benefits other sentient beings is dependent on the attitude and receptivity of others. Obviously, the Buddha and his followers developed infinite altruism, boundless love and compassion that was very powerful. But in our practice of compassion, we cannot be sure if it is going to benefit others or not. Sometimes, if you are trying to smile at someone or somehow to express genuine affection, people become suspicious! But as far as the practitioner himself or herself is concerned, as soon as the altruistic attitude develops, there is immense benefit.

To think the practice of compassion is something good only for others is wrong. I feel that when you practice caring for others, ultimately, you get the maximum benefit. Sometimes I jokingly tell my audience, "Oh, these bodhisattvas, they are truly selfish! They always think about others." Many of our difficulties and troubles are, I think, related to our mental projections. If someone's mental attitude is right, even when surrounded by a hostile environment, that person can be peaceful and happy. Lama Tsongkhapa has aptly remarked on this.

When we talk about the practice of perfections, particularly the practice of the six perfections, and try to find the relevance of these personal practices to others, we discover what is known as gathering disciplines for maturing one's mind. This means that through the practice of the six perfections, there is a direct connection to helping others. However, if you examine practices like concentration and the development of wisdom-realizing emptiness, you realize that these are meditations and techniques to improve or enhance one's wisdom and one's realization.

When we refer to the practice of morality, it is a kind of self-purification method. When we talk about giving, we do not refer to the elimination of poverty of others through giving, but to a mental state in which you are always ready to give your body, wealth, and pleasures when others need them. It really doesn't mean that you are able to solve the problems and poverty of other people. The practice of giving and generosity is meant to enhance one's wish to give to others. This way, you improve and enhance your courage and determination to offer yourself to the service of others.

Regarding the practice of giving and generosity, there are three levels of giving, determined by their quality. The first level is called "giving material facilities." The second is "giving fearlessness," that is, protecting others from suffering and fear. And the third level is called "giving dharma teaching." Regarding the practice of giving material facilities, there are two types. One is offering external material facilities, and the second is offering internal physical facilities, for example, offering one's eye or one's limbs. When it comes to implementing the practice of giving, be it giving external material facilities or giving parts of your body, it is important to find out whether it is the right time to give. You should carefully examine the object or person to whom you are making these gifts, the time concerned, and your motivation. Also, you should examine the article being given. For example, it is not permitted to offer poison or weapons.

Generally, something like medicine is considered suitable to offer to others. However, in certain circumstances, in relation to specific people, giving medicine may be harmful rather than helpful, and the practice would be discouraged. Offering food is usually suitable and welcomed. But if you offer food to someone who is fasting, it is improper. Therefore, when you undertake the practice of giving and generosity, it is important to analyze and examine everything about the situation.

Where the practice of morality is concerned, particularly in the context of a bodhisattva practice, there are three types of morality. The first is called the "morality refraining from engaging in negative deeds." The second is the "morality collecting virtuous qualities." And the third is called the "morality of fulfilling the purposes of sentient beings." The three kinds of morality are linked. In order to develop the third morality, you need to develop the second morality. Unless you have the necessary virtuous qualities, it is not possible to help others. In order to develop these qualities, you need to have developed the first morality. Unless you eliminate or avoid afflictive emotions, it is not possible to develop virtuous qualities.

With regard to the practice of patience, these are of three types. The first is the "patience of being able to bear hardships and sufferings." The second is the "patience of voluntarily welcoming sufferings and hardships." And the third is the "patience of developing ascertainment toward dharma practices," which refers to meditating on emptiness.

There are divisions in the perfection of effort and concentration, but I do not remember them! However, in the case of concentration, there is one level which is related to the practice of conventional truth, and there is concentration which is related to the practice of the view of emptiness.

In considering wisdom, we can say there are two main kinds of wisdom: one which is called "wisdom realizing the conventional phenomena," and the other called "wisdom realizing the ultimate reality, ultimate truth." Calm abiding meditation or special insight are distinguished not by whether the object is a conventional truth or an ultimate truth but on how the mind focuses on the object.

So, this is the end of the six perfections. The practices of the six perfections can be summarized under the practice of two: method (for collecting merit) and wisdom (for collecting wisdom). We categorize the six perfections into the practices of method and wisdom by putting the practices of concentration and wisdom under the collection of wisdom; and the practice of giving, the observance of morality, and a part of the practice of patience under the collection of merit. With regard to the practice of effort, one part of it is included in the accumulation of merit and the other in the accumulation of wisdom.

Effort is applicable to accumulating merit as well as wisdom. The practices regarding these are the two main causes which are responsible for actualizing the form body of the Buddha and the truth body of the Buddha. The division of the path into method and wisdom is related to the fundamental reality of the object because, in the law of nature, we see two categories of phenomena. One is conventional phenomena, and the other is the ultimate reality of those phenomena. We talk about two truths, conventional truth and ultimate truth.

For a proper understanding of these two truths, it is important to understand the disparity between appearances and reality.

We have different types of appearances, on the one hand, and, on the other, we have a reality which is different from those appearances. Therefore, I feel that when we undertake any kind of learning process, what we are trying to do is to reduce the disparity, the distance or the gap between appearance and reality.

We try to know reality through education, particularly through analytical forces, including experiments. We are not satisfied with appearances. Education and investigation help to reduce the gap between appearances and reality. The concept of two truths is of tremendous help in reducing this gap. Because many negative emotions develop on the basis of appearances, realizing reality reduces negative emotions. So that's why the concept of shunya is very relevant to daily experiences. If these concepts just remain on the intellectual level, as mere information, they will have little effect.

Your Holiness, someone has asked about the cause of terrorism. Can counterviolence subjugate terrorist activities? And what is the role of compassion in this world of terror that has led to the violent clash of civilizations?

Certainly, I think the root of terrorism is hatred, short-sightedness, and narrow-mindedness. I think the countermeasure should be on two levels. One, an immediate method or countermeasure. And the other for the long run. So, I think all leaders and the people concerned should make every effort to find nonviolent ways to deal with the situation. This is my wish, my prayer. Otherwise, I have no idea how these things can be handled because mental states, emotions, will be out of control. In the long run, I think our whole world and society must become more compassionate. Then, when we find disagreement or conflict, we will look for peaceful responses and peaceful resolutions through dialogue. I think we can do that. Eventually, we can produce a more compassionate society. Of course, this is not easy, but, I think, it is possible.

Some say, in general, Westerners don't progress as quickly on the Vajrayana path as the Tibetans do. Would you agree? If yes, why?

In the Tibetan society as well, even though there are many who practice tantra, there are very few who have the realization as explained in the tantric texts. As I mentioned earlier, it is partly because of a lack of seriousness as it is done as a daily routine. You recite certain prayers and practice in a routine manner. Of course, this is my impression. So I do not think there is much of a difference between Westerners and Easterners. They are the same.

How important is the method and its selection that will lead us to a higher level of spirituality?

That is extremely important. Because if you are able to follow a method and select a path which is relevant and suitable to your mental disposition, it will be much more effective. With regard to the previous question on the practice of tantra, tantric or Vajrayana practice is a Mahayana practice and, therefore, has to be influenced by the development of bodhicitta and wisdom-discerning emptiness. In the absence of these two—development of bodhicitta and wisdom-realizing emptiness—it is impossible to undertake a tantric practice. Some people have the impression that Hinayana, Mahayana, and Vajrayana are different yanas, or vehicles, and are quite independent of one another. That is absolutely wrong.

One should realize that in order to practice

Bodhisattvayana, also called Mahayana, the foundation of the practice is based on the teaching of the Four Noble Truths and the Eightfold Path. On that foundation, the bodhisattva's practice is built. Therefore, in the absence of these fundamental practices taught in the Hinayana or Theravada tradition, it is not possible to construct the Mahayana practices. In the absence of the Mahayana sutrayana practices, it is not possible to undertake a Mahayana tantric practice. The higher level spiritual practices are built on the foundation of the preceding practices.

Hindus speak of Brahma, the impersonal god beyond all attributes and descriptions. Enlightenment is becoming one with Brahma. Although Buddhists do not acknowledge a god, could Buddha nature not be thought of as the Buddhist equivalent of Brahma?

If you try, you could interpret it in that way to some extent. In the Christian tradition, the Trinity is sometimes said to be similar to the Buddhist notion of Buddha, Dharma, and Sangha, or with the three kayas: dharmakaya, sambhoghakaya, and nirmanakaya. We can recognize some similarities. It does not matter.

If liberation, too, is a result of causation, how can bad become good?

The bad can become good because we can put an end to the continuity of bad activities. Now, here I think the being, the sentient being which has feeling or cognitive power that is always there according to Bodhisattvayana or especially in the Madhyamika philosophical viewpoint, that is beginningless. Mind, subtle mind, is beginningless. In Lama Tsongkhapa's great tantric stages of the path, he cites a quotation from one explanatory tantra, called Vajra Shekhara, which says that the cyclic existence is a continuum of tantra and that nirvana is a subsequent tantra. When we talk about cyclic existence or nirvana, it has to be explained in connection with the continuum of tantra, that is, the continuity of the mind. But so long as there is a continuity of mind and the impure or afflicted emotions remain, that is samsara. When all the negative or afflicted emotions—due to their antidotes—are eliminated, that mind is said to be in the state of nirvana.

In the case of nirvana itself, it is unconditioned, not dependent on causes and conditions. According to the philosophical viewpoint of Prasangika Madhyamika, the system of Nagarjuna and Chandrakirti, when we talk about nirvana, we refer to the ultimate state, the ultimate reality of the mind, when the mind is totally purified of the afflictive emotions.

I am very unhappy to see my neighbors happy. I know it is wrong but how do I overcome this? I want my child to be the best. Is it wrong?

Do you like friends or not? I think most people love friends. If you have friends, genuine friends, with whom you can exchange smiles and different experiences with trust, you feel much happier, much calmer. If you distrust everybody, you feel lonely and have a sense of insecurity. Therefore, there is at least a chance that your neighbor can become your friend. Is it not better to have a neighbor who is your friend rather than a neighbor who is your enemy? Whether someone becomes a friend or an enemy depends on your mental attitude. First you have to extend your hand and show friendship. Then there is a chance that eventually attitudes will change. If you remain negative toward someone, becoming friends is impossible.

Friends, genuine friends, have much to do with a warm heart, not money, not power. When you gain wealth, political power, or fame, you may find friends of a different sort—but these are not necessarily genuine friends. A genuine friend considers you just as another human being, as a brother or sister, and shows affection on that level, regardless of whether you are rich or poor, in a high position or a low position. That is a genuine friend.

Your Holiness talked about helping others in their suffering. In that context, what do you feel about euthanasia or increasing the dosage of morphine when someone is dying?

In general, it is much better not to practice euthanasia, but there could be exceptions.

What should the attitude of the students be toward acquiring knowledge?

I don't know. You need to take the initiative and make some effort.

In general, when we acquire knowledge, there are three levels of processes: hearing, thinking, then meditation. So, mere hearing and the knowledge that comes from just hearing is very shallow. One has to think for oneself and, if possible, experiment, make further investigations, analyze further. In that way, you gain a deeper awareness. Then your knowledge is much sounder and, eventually, can be transformed into action. If this question were asked by a Buddhist, in particular by a Tibetan Buddhist, I would add that you should recite the mantra of Manshjushri, *om ah ra pa dsa na dhi.* If you recite this, it will help your intelligence. In my case, since my childhood I have been reciting this mantra—whether it really helps or not, I don't know. But definitely it does no harm.

Is there any possibility of a global religion for all the people of the world?

No, it is not possible. I think a "global religion" could mean warm human hearts, affection, a sense of caring, and altruistic minds. This could be a global religion. Other than that, I see the different traditions remaining. They are useful for such a wide variety of humanity. Just one religion . . . I do not think there is much benefit in that.

Is the theory of karma valid? Is all that happens predetermined?

Karma does not have the connotation of "predetermined." By depending on different levels of actions, one can change the course of one's experience of life. I'm giving an example from our daily life: in the morning, you plan something, you want to take a certain action, maybe, carry out plans that were fixed last week, but then some emergency occurs, and everything changes. Although the result of a certain action is programmed, if some more forceful action comes, the results will change.

Why are so many young people getting heart problems?

I think because of tension. Also, less inner strength and too many expectations from outside. And, also, too much ambition. Perhaps, behavior problems, drugs and alcohol. Better to ask a doctor!

Your Holiness, many people feel very possessive about you. How do you handle this?

You can become possessive, but that does not make much of a difference to me.

I am just sitting here.

But Your Holiness, it creates problems for others.

If it creates problems, they should stop being possessive. There was a similar question once in Germany. There I said that I consider myself made up of the elements of earth, wind, water, and fire. In whatever way others can benefit from me, may they enjoy!

Sir Shankerlal Hall, Modern School, 2002

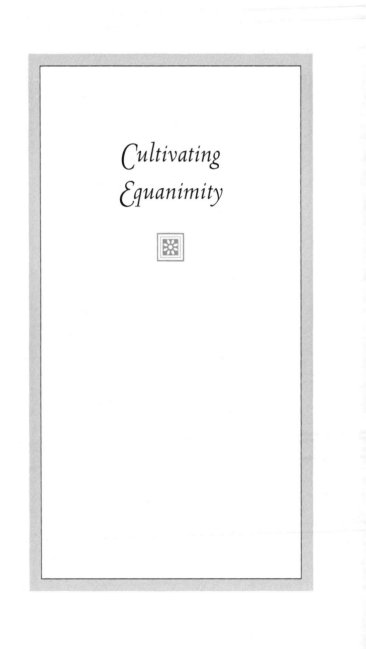

Cultivating
Equanimity

Time never waits or remains still; it is always moving. When I look back over the last two decades as a Buddhist monk and as a practitioner, I feel that I have had very little spiritual development. However, on a more careful consideration, I realize that through a constant familiarization with altruism, with the help of wisdom, and with some analytical meditation on shunyata, there has been, comparatively, some change and improvement. Even a minuscule spiritual development is progress, and I think this is of immense benefit in sustaining the peace of mind. This, in turn, has a positive impact on health. So, any amount of mental development is useful.

A Dharma Celebration is not a mere social

gathering. It is a reminder that in human life, spirituality is important; it matters. The word *dharma*, the Sanskrit word, has a comprehensive meaning. In the case of Dharma Celebration, *dharma* means Buddha Dharma. The essential feature of Buddha Dharma is to maximize the utilization of human intelligence so as to develop an effective way to transform our emotions. That is the unique thing about Buddha Dharma.

All major religions aim to transform emotions as they are crucial factors in our lives. Negative and painful experiences affect our emotions. Transformation means preserving positive emotions or, in some cases, strengthening positive emotions and reducing negative ones. As I said earlier, I think all major religious traditions show concern for the transformation of emotions. But their methods for doing so are not the same. In many traditions, the transformation of emotions occurs mainly through faith, which is powerful and important.

A strong faith in God or Allah, in Lord Krishna or Shiva, or in Jesus Christ can certainly impact on one's emotions. After all, the message of all these great masters is basically the same: one of love, compassion, forgiveness, tolerance, discipline, and contentment. These are the basics of all these traditions. But in the Buddhist tradition, we not only have faith or trust in the Buddha, we must also investigate the Buddha. How do we do this? The Buddha, the historical Buddha, is already gone. The only way to find out is to examine his teachings and to inquire about the Buddha's devout followers. If we thoroughly investigate their thinking and behavior, we may eventually know the kind of impact the Buddha's teachings can have. Also, through learning the teachings and trying to emulate them in our experiences, we can, eventually, develop some kind of conviction. That conviction does not come from mere faith but through our investigation while using our intelligence.

Wisdom is not mere knowledge; it is knowledge first through hearing, second through analyzing the meaning through reason, and then connecting it to our experiences. Finally, comes firm conviction. Altruism is found in all traditions, but the combination of altruism with wisdom or intelligence is unique to Buddha Dharma. When I say unique, I do not mean that Buddha Dharma is the best. The question of which dharma is the best is difficult to answer. It is like food. We cannot say one particular kind of food is the best. Food is related to different physical states and to the different tastes of individuals who relish it. For some people, Indian spices are extremely hot and too spicy. For others, they are delicious. Judging what is the best has to be made according to one's particular circumstances. Similarly, I think, asserting which religion is the best must be based on the benefit gained by each individual practitioner.

So, as far as the religious aspect is concerned, I believe all traditions are more or less the same. All of them are concerned with human happiness and goodness. All religious teachings try to promote or strengthen positive human values. That aspect is basically the same in all traditions. However, the philosophical aspect is another vital part of religious traditions. Here we find that there are vast differences. Buddha Dharma, especially the tradition of Nalanda, is very sophisticated and subtle. I think, as far as the philosophical background is concerned, Buddhism is very rich. Within the Buddha Dharma, the Pali and the Sanskrit traditions are philosophically the most sophisticated.

I feel the best way to introduce the Tibetan Buddha Dharma is through the Nalanda tradition, because all the major texts are known. For example, at the age of six or seven I started—with great reluctance—to learn those texts by heart. When we study all the major texts written by the Nalanda masters like Nagarjuna, Arya Asanga, Chandrakirti, and so on, in their entirety, as a whole stretch of Buddha Dharma, we can see that the Nalanda tradition has contributed greatly to the philosophical aspect of Buddha Dharma. The ritualistic part, where the Tibetans play cymbals and blow huge horns, is not from Nalanda. Some of these ceremonial, ritual instruments, I think, came from Afghanistan and China.

To return to my point—we can develop conviction through utilizing our human intelligence in the maximum way possible and through our compassion. Conviction brings enthusiasm which, in turn, brings hard work. We become used to virtuous practices, and this has a great impact on our emotional world. That is the Buddhist way. When people ask questions about the easiest way or the best way, I have difficulty answering them. I think one often asks such questions about the simplest or the easiest out of laziness or lack of courage. These questions are okay if, for example, you are cooking. You can then ask about the easiest way, or perhaps the cheapest way. But as far as the transformation of our emotions is concerned, these questions are irrelevant. Look at Buddha Shakyamuni, our teacher. It is recounted clearly that he undertook three eons of practice to achieve the state of enlightenment. And our Nalanda masters—

siddhas like Tilopa and Naropa, and the Tibetan masters like Milarepa and Tsongkhapa—spent many years in remote areas bearing innumerable hardships in order to transform their emotions.

The human emotions that we experience today and want to transform are the same as those that existed about two thousand years ago or three thousand years ago. If we compare human emotions that existed several hundred thousand years ago or one million years ago with the current ones, we will see some differences in them because of our increased intelligence. In the future, if we survive another few hundred thousand years, maybe human emotions will be different. We can change our state of mind or emotion if we utilize our intelligence and are guided by people like Nagarjuna and Shantideva. If developing an altruistic mind is our goal, I think that Shantideva's book is the best. For understanding the ultimate reality, Nagarjuna's *Madhyamakamulakarika* is among the best, and so is Chandrakirti's *Madhyamakavatara*.

Generally speaking, in today's world, our acceptance of one another is improving. As a person who believes in religious and spiritual values, I think harmony and unity are essential. These values will come if we respect each other. Genuine respect will come if we have more contact with one another and come to understand one another's values. We must develop admiration and appreciation for each other. All religious traditions, over a period of many centuries, have made immense contributions to developing human values and peace of mind. They have given hope and inspiration to millions of people, and that's quite sufficient to earn our admiration.

However, as I mentioned earlier, we are still experiencing problems among people of different religions. Such tragic events show that we need a sustained effort to face new challenges. We can't blame one individual for what happens in our world. I think we should blame our entire society. Society produces our leaders and politicians, and if we try to develop a more compassionate and affectionate society, we will have human beings with a more peaceful nature. Leaders, politicians, and businesspeople coming from such a society would offer hope for a better world. Our long-term responsibility—everyone's responsibility, whether they are believers or nonbelievers—is to find ways to promote a peaceful and compassionate society.

I think one way is quite simple. Each individual must try to ensure peace and compassion in his family. Put together ten peaceful, compassionate homes, or one hundred, and that's a community.

The children in such a society would receive affection in their family and in their schools from the educators concerned. We might have one or two setbacks, but generally I think we could develop a sensible society. Sensible here means a sense of community, a sense of responsibility, and a sense of commitment.

Now, about equanimity. What disturbs our mind is, primarily, afflictive emotions like hatred and attachment. And one of the antidotes that can alleviate and reduce such emotions is the practice of equanimity. Here, we are not talking about equanimity with no presence of feeling or with indifference. We mean sensitivity to experiences of the positive and the negative and being able to distinguish between right and wrong. One should adopt a way of life in which one cherishes positive values and tries to shun negative ones. We are talking about equanimity in the sense of alleviating attachment and hatred.

I feel that equanimity can be practiced both by someone with a religious viewpoint and by someone who does not adhere to any particular religious tradition. It's the same with the cultivation of positive qualities like love and compassion: they can be based on reasoning and understanding from a particular religious tradition, or can be developed without any religious basis. An individual practitioner can develop loving-kindness and compassion by thinking that through such practices, he or she will achieve enlightenment because the Buddha taught this path. On the other hand, a person could develop such qualities thinking that the development of love and compassion would bring mental peace, physical well-being, or harmony and peace within his or her family. This kind of reasoning is not based on any religious tradition.

In developing equanimity, one needs to understand that negative emotions like hatred and attachment are improper and not healthy because they are biased and partial. When one's mind is partial, one will not be able to see reality and will not be objective. With this kind of understanding, one can strengthen equanimity. Many of the problems that we encounter and the difficulties that we face are because we are not able to see reality clearly. A biased mental attitude or partiality is a big hindrance and an obstruction to comprehending reality. For example, the reality is that things are dependent on multifarious causes and factors: things are interconnected, interdependent and interrelated. When we are unable to see this reality, then problems arise because we tend to pick out just one factor—whether it is the experience of happiness or that of problems and difficulties—and try to use it to explain a complex situation. We tend to highlight just one factor out of the many and focus exclusively on that particular cause or factor. Because of this, we are unable to solve many issues confronting us. In fact, instead of solving difficulties, we sometimes create additional ones.

To deal effectively with a particular problem, it is important to prepare ourselves mentally to understand the reality of a situation and to be able to see facts objectively. One of the main factors which hinders us from seeing the objectivity of a situation is the partiality of the mind and its biased state. You can see why practicing equanimity is very important. Also, common sense is needed to handle difficult situations. When we confront complex situations and try to solve the problems inherent in them, it is important to have a holistic attitude rather than a narrow mind. Particularly in today's world, such a holistic attitude is important. If you focus only on the interests of your family and forget others, or if you focus only on the interests of your nation and forget the rest of the nations, it will be impossible to achieve long-lasting peace and happiness. If you let afflictive emotions control your mind, your mind will become biased and partial; it will be lopsided, one-sided. Then you will not be able to develop a holistic approach.

For those who accept religious traditions, we see that they fall in two different categories. One centers on faith in a creator; the other—including Buddhism, Jainism and a part of the Samkhya tradition—centers on self-creation. For someone who accepts the creator, God, there is ample opportunity to develop a sense of equanimity. When one understands that everything is created by God, then one sees all creatures as coming from one ultimate source. For the development of equanimity, this view is particularly useful when one confronts a so-called troublemaker, an enemy. Normally, we label a person or a group of people as an "enemy" when, under particular circumstances, they create problems for us. But if we see the person from a wider perspective and realize that he or she is a part of humanity and a part of God's creation, our negative feelings will diminish. This view could be helpful in the development of equanimity.

Sometimes I think we religious people, including myself, choose to take those concepts that suit us and forget those that are not comfortable. To those who believe in God or in a creator, I ask them to put more emphasis on the equality of all human beings. Forget about other galaxies and concentrate on this globe, this planet. If one creator created all earthly beings, discrimination has no place. There can be no differences on the basis of color, social background, or, particularly in this country, of caste.

According to ancient Indian thought, the role of karma is essential in the practice of equanimity, and Buddhism shares this view. Here, equanimity means not developing great attachment to one thing and, simultaneously, not developing hatred toward another. In ancient Indian thought, the development of this kind of equanimity is based on an understanding of the concept of karma. This concept implies that everything we are today, the positive and negative thoughts we have, and the different aspects and expressions that we make, are a result of what we did in our past. Once we develop such an understanding, we will handle more easily our encounters with others— even unpleasant ones. We will realize that what the person we are encountering is expressing right now is a result of his or her karma. We are able to blame the negative karma rather than blaming the individual person. In this way, we are able to develop equanimity. Also, the old Indian belief in the existence of past lives and future lives helps in encounters with the so-called enemies in this life. Instead of thinking that a particular person is creating problems for us, we focus on the point that in the past, he or she may have been our best friend or a close relative. Then it is not easy to label her or him as an enemy.

In the Buddha Dharma, particularly in the Mahayana tradition or the Sanskrit tradition, all sentient beings have a Buddha nature. So when we face problems dealing with other people, we remember that they are sentient beings just like us and have a Buddha nature. The ultimate nature of everyone is pure. This belief will calm our mind and will reduce negative feelings.

Another powerful method of attaining equanimity is developing the realization that you want happiness—the maximum happiness, the best kind of happiness. You do not want suffering and are unable to tolerate even the tiniest problem or the smallest amount of suffering. Just as you have this inborn wish about happiness and suffering, so does everyone else. You should be able to understand that these aspirations are present in everybody.

In the Buddhist practice, when we talk about developing equanimity, we refer to two levels. On the first level, we understand that we should not develop a special attachment to one group of people and hatred toward another. Instead, we develop a state of mental equilibrium. Some of the examples I have given illustrate the process of developing equanimity on this level, that is, reaching a point where you do not have any special attachment to one group and hatred toward another. These examples point to things being interconnected, to everyone being influenced by afflictive emotions, and to the law of karma causing everyone to suffer.

On the second level of equanimity, we wish to benefit everyone regardless of the feelings of distance or closeness. To develop this, we reflect on the fact that everybody, just like ourselves, wants happiness and does not want suffering. We try to remember that we all are of a similar nature and have the same urges and longings. To help and benefit other sentient beings, we do not segregate them. We do not make distinctions among them. Without feeling distant and without feeling close, we can develop a powerful mind, wishing to benefit everyone without differentiation. We can strengthen this practice of equanimity by reflecting on the destructive results of a self-cherishing attitude and the positive results of altruism and cherishing the welfare of other sentient beings. To reduce a self-cherishing attitude and to develop altruism, one should read *Bodhicharyavatara* by Shantideva. Here, we find numerous examples of why such practices should be done and how they can be developed. If we study and reflect on the teachings in the *Bodhicharyavatara* and on the problems and conflicts in the world today, we can easily understand the benefits of altruism and the harm of self-cherishing.

The meditation on emptiness is useful in the development of equanimity. To understand how this meditation helps, reflect on how the afflictive emotions harm us. For example, think of the destructive results of anger or hatred. When we develop anger and hatred, it not only destroys peace in the minds of other people, it also harms us greatly. Hatred and anger usually take aggressive forms and are expressed in violent ways. However, when we reflect on other kinds of afflictive emotions like attachment, they seem to be gentle and appear to us as friends. But they also are very destructive.

When we develop attachment, it could be relating to possessions—for example, this belongs to me or he belongs to me—and it could also refer to yourself, the "I" that you think is you. The attachment to the "I" arises because you perceive yourself as something concrete, objective, and existing on its own. It is because of this strong adherence to the solidity of oneself that other attachments develop. Similarly, when you develop hatred, you tend to see the object of your hate as something independent and concrete. For example, let us say that you are angry with a certain Mr. Gupta. If you are angry with Mr. Gupta and think that he is stupid and silly, at that very point, you are seeing him as an object. You are seeing Mr. Gupta as existing on his own, as being independent and concrete. But if you pause and ask, "Where is this Mr. Gupta? Who is he? Is Mr. Gupta his mind or his body?" If you do a little bit of analysis, you will see that it is impossible to pinpoint him. And when you are unable to identify that which you thought existed concretely, your tight grasping is relaxed. Similarly, when you get greatly attached to one particular person, if you pause and ask the same questions, you will find that you are unable to pinpoint a concretely existing person. Again, this relaxes your strong grasping. The same holds true if you analyze the strong grasping you have for yourself as an individual "I."

If you pause and ask, "Where is this 'I'? Where is this 'me' toward which I have such a strong grasping?" you won't be able to find it. That will lead you to wonder how you could have developed such a strong grasping toward something you cannot even identify. In this way, by seeing your selflessness, you can reduce the intensity of afflictive emotions like hatred and attachment. When we talk about selflessness, it does not mean the nonexistence of the self. Rather, it means that there is no self with an objective, independent nature.

With regard to developing an antidote to reduce self-grasping, we can look at the meanings of selflessness in different Buddhist systems. In Buddhist thought, we talk of reflecting on the meaning of the selflessness of all phenomena. Here, we are not talking about selflessness as the lack of the inherent existence of a person. We are talking about it in reference to the object being used and employed by the person. Whether it is the object being enjoyed, or the person that enjoys the object, the reality is the same: there is no independent inherent existence. This view of selflessness is expounded in the Mind-Only, or Cittamatra, school of thought. According to this school, there is no externally existent object. Everything is the creation of the mind: everything is in the mind. You do not experience any object that is substantially separate from the mind.

Take the example of employing a sense-consciousness, our vision. When the sense-consciousness of the eye focuses on a particular object, say a flower, the Cittamatra school explains that the object appears to us as having a solid,

independent existence, irrespective of the impu-
tations made by the mind. They say that when a
particular sense-consciousness, like the eye sense-
consciousness, engages an object, three appearances
or three modes of perception arise. The first is seeing the flower as a flower. The second is to see the
flower as the basis of language, as the basis of the
engagement of the name, the flower. The third is
to see that flower as having an inherent or objective
existence from its own side; you not only see the
flower as the object of the application of a name,
but you also see the object as having an inherent
existence. When the Cittamatra school explains
these three levels of perception, they say that they
arise through the activation of three types of imprints. About seeing the flower as the flower, for
example, they say that you are able to see the
flower as the flower because of the activation of a
concordant imprint, a similar type of imprint.

According to the Mind-Only school of thought,
there is nothing that has an external existence;
everything is substantially the same with the mind.
However, when we relate to an object like a flower,
we can see it in three different ways. And when we
see the flower as having an independent existence,
we are mistaken. If you tried to defend this mistaken understanding, you might do so by saying

that there is a flower substantially separate from the sense-consciousness because you can see the flower existing outside the sense-consciousness. The Mind-Only school of thought responds by saying that your seeing the flower as substantially separate from the mind is because of the awakening of the wrong imprints, imprints left behind by one's self-grasping in past lives. In this way, they conclude that there are no externally existent objects. The flower and the mind that perceives the flower are substantially the same.

Now we will consider the Madhyamika school of thought. It challenges the Cittamatra school by saying, "Yes, your perspective of seeing everything as substantially the same as the mind will help reduce the development of attachment and aversion to external objects, but how about the mind itself? How would you reduce attachment and hatred toward the mind itself?" The Madhyamika school holds that the external object and the internal mind are equal; neither has an inherent existence. If things existed independently, there would be no disparity or gap between appearance and reality. However, in our lives, we encounter innumerable experiences of disparity between appearance and reality. Thus, no distinction can be made between the object and the mind. Selflessness is presented in this way by the Madhyamika school of thought. By developing this understanding of selflessness, you will be able to recognize that since there is no object and no subjective mind to pinpoint and hold, there is no basis on which to develop grasping.

The Buddha taught what is known as the four Buddhist promulgations or four Buddhist seals: all conditioned phenomena are impermanent; all contaminated things are suffering; all phenomena are selfless and empty; and nirvana or liberation is peace. By understanding these Buddhist promulgations, you can reach different stages of equanimity. For example, in understanding the first teaching that all conditional phenomena are impermanent, you realize that all things are caused, and that they are all transitory and impermanent. By understanding that all conditional phenomena are on the same level since they are impermanent, you can develop equanimity. It is from this perspective that Shantideva's *Bodhicharyavatara* asks how an impermanent thing can develop hatred toward another which is also impermanent and equally transitory. Similarly, the second teaching, which says that all contaminated things are suffering, means that just as my mind is contaminated and polluted and suffering is part of my nature, the same applies to all other people. Then I must ask, how can I hate or get attached to other beings when we are all the same.

Understanding that all phenomena are selfless and empty leads to the same conclusion. When we talk of nirvana as peace, or liberation as the state of total peace, we realize that everyone possesses a Buddha nature and can easily develop equanimity.

So, to build equanimity, we must first gain knowledge, and then, through our awareness and experiences, develop conviction. That is the proper way to practice. Eventually, the impact on our emotions will be felt.

Is there a difference between the clear light mind and the Buddha nature?

They are the same. The Buddha nature can be the empty nature of the mind, in which case it is not a consciousness. It can also refer to the primordial clear light mind which is more related to the tantric teaching.

Is Vipassana meditation the only way to enlightenment?

It depends on what you mean by enlightenment. On one level, we think of an enlightened mind as being more sophisticated or wiser. But I think enlightenment has various levels. Also, Vipassana has many varieties and while some forms are helpful in achieving some forms of enlightenment, it is difficult to say, without reservation, that through Vipassana one can achieve enlightenment. This is a difficult question.

Why is the power of evil greater than that of goodness?

I do not think this is true. The power of evil is sometimes very powerful, but only temporarily. In the long run, I don't think it is more powerful than goodness.

Ego and self-respect are two conflicting emotions inherent in human nature. How can the common man extract the positive values from these two feelings using equanimity?

First, I don't think of ego and self-respect as being necessarily contradictory terms. When we think of developing positive qualities like bodhicitta or altruism, we realize that we need a strong sense of ego and self-respect. I suppose we could say there are two kinds of ego. One is positive. An example of this is when you develop your ego, thinking that you must achieve enlightenment to be able to benefit all suffering sentient beings. One of my favorite prayers is, "So long as space remains, I will remain." Here, you need a strong sense of I, a strong ego in order to be useful to others. But the negative ego is the extreme self-centered I. That ego leads to the harm and exploitation of others.

Who is the creator, who created the creator, and why?

For Buddhists, that is the problem: how did a creator occur? That is why Buddhists do not accept a creator. But, of course, as I mentioned earlier, we respect the concept and its importance to others.

If you do not develop attachment, how will relationships grow?

Friendship and attachment are different things. One of my friends, a Chilean nuclear scientist, once told me that when you engage in any scientific field of study and analysis, you must remain very objective. You should be completely engaged in analysis, but, at the same time, you should be detached. That applies here as well.

What is the most important thing we can do to attain world peace and tolerance?

I think achieving world peace will take time. It must begin at the most basic levels, with individuals and with families, and grow from there.

How can we differentiate between idiot compassion and generosity?

The question is not clear. What is meant by idiot compassion?

Your Holiness, it means being compassionate blindly, without intention.

So, actually, idiot compassion is not compassion at all.

What is your message for politicians of the world?

Be truthful. Be honest.

Can a common man with family responsibilities achieve nirvana or Buddhahood?

Oh, yes, no question about it.

How can we find true happiness?

From the Buddhist point of view, the highest form of peace is true cessation or nirvana. That state of true cessation is not a fleeting mental experience. Once you achieve it, you gain long-lasting, stable peace and happiness.

How can Buddhists help the Tibetan cause in India and in the West?

Today, among the Chinese, there is growing interest in dharma, in general, and in Tibetan Buddhism in particular. In the long run, this is a very positive factor for Tibetan issues. So we must make clear what the Tibetan Buddhist tradition actually is. It is the pure tradition of Nalanda. Many Indians are aware that Nalanda is a center of learning, a place for the development of intellectual traditions. Unfortunately, Tibetan Buddhism is sometimes presented in its superficial aspects, with masks and countless rituals. In this, I think there is a real danger of misunderstanding Buddha Dharma. If we clearly explain that the Tibetan tradition is a continuity of the pure Nalanda tradition, misconceptions will not arise.

Who can serve beings better? A tenth-ground bodhisattva or a buddha?

The question has some element of silliness. If a bodhisattva on the tenth ground has the level of capacity that would allow a direct comparison with a buddha, the very question of becoming enlightened further does not arise. However, it is said that a bodhisattva on the tenth ground has achieved a level on which he can serve sentient beings in a manner quite comparable to the state of Buddhahood.

Compared to bodhisattvas on the first nine grounds, a bodhisattva on the tenth ground is at the highest level and is called a bodhisattva bhumi. After this is the stage of the achievement of enlightenment, and special respect is shown to this bodhisattva level. Sometimes even the name "the bhumi of the Buddha" is given.

Your Holiness, when people fall sick, they undergo tremendous shock and lose their equanimity. We are interested to know what His Holiness experienced when he was unwell.

I was in Bihar, one of the poorest states. While I was passing through Nalanda, Rajgir, Bodhgaya, and Patna, I saw many poor people, especially children and old people, many of whom were very sick. It seemed no one was taking care of them. In a hotel in Patna, I became ill and experienced extreme pain. But, mentally, I began reflecting on the poor people I had seen earlier, especially the children. Somehow, my mind was diverted from my own pain. That's an example of practicing compassion and having a sense of caring for others that benefits oneself immensely. One's own pain is somehow forgotten.

Normally, when there is a gathering of Buddhists, we recite three verses for the generation of bodhicitta and reflect on their meaning.

The first verse refers to taking refuge in the Buddha, the Dharma, and the Sangha. The second refers to generating bodhicitta or altruism. And the third refers to strengthening and enhancing the bodhisattva practices. Normally, when I confer a short ceremony for the development of bodhicitta, I base it on these verses.

You should visualize, first of all, that while in the presence of a thangka or an image of the Buddha, you are in the actual presence of the Buddha Shakyamuni. Then, in the display of the other thangkas representing the six ornaments and the two Supremes, you imagine that you are seeing the eight great spiritual masters of Nalanda. Imagine that these are not just images of thangkas, but mean the actual presence of these masters. And imagine that in front of the presence of Buddha and these great, highly accomplished masters, you are taking refuge, generating bodhicitta for the benefit of all suffering sentient beings.

For those of you belonging to other traditions, you can reflect on the teacher of your faith.

Recite these verses three times. I have referred to them earlier also. Their power never fails.

> With a wish to free all beings
> I shall always go for refuge
> To the Buddha, Dharma, and Sangha
> Until I reach full enlightenment.
>
> Enthused by wisdom and compassion
> Today in the Buddha's presence
> I generate the mind for full awakening
> For the benefit of all sentient beings.

Cultivating Equanimity

As long as space remains
As long as sentient beings remain
Until then, may I, too, remain
And dispel the miseries of the world.

Talkatora Indoor Stadium, 2003

*The Four
Noble Truths
and the
Eight Verses
of Thought
Transformation*

When the great teacher Shakyamuni Buddha first spoke about the dharma in India, he taught the Four Noble Truths: the truths of suffering, the cause of suffering, the cessation of suffering, and the path to the cessation of suffering. Since many books contain discussions of the Four Noble Truths (and the Eightfold Path), they are well known. These four are all-encompassing.

Speaking of the Four Noble Truths in general, and considering that all of us want to achieve happiness and eliminate suffering, we can speak of an effect and a cause on both the disturbing side and the liberating side. While true sufferings and the true causes of suffering are the effect and cause of things that we do not want, the true cessation and the true paths are the effect and cause of things that we desire.

✦

We experience many different kinds of suffering. They are included in three categories: the suffering of suffering, the suffering of change, and the all-pervasive suffering.

Suffering of suffering: This refers to things like headaches. Even animals can recognize this kind of suffering and, like us, want to be free from it. As beings are afraid of, and experience discomfort from, these kinds of suffering, they undertake various activities to eliminate them.

Suffering of change: This refers to situations where, for example, we are sitting, comfortably relaxed, and at first everything is all right, but after a while we get restless and feel uncomfortable.

In certain countries like India, we see a great deal of poverty and disease: these are sufferings of the first category. Everybody realizes that these are sufferings—conditions to be eliminated and improved upon. In many Western countries, there may not be so much poverty, but even in places where material facilities occur in plenty, there are different kinds of problems. At first, we may be very happy, having overcome the problems that our forefathers faced, but as soon as we have solved certain problems, new ones arise. We have plenty of money, food, and a good shelter, but by overestimating the value of these things, we render them worthless. This sort of experience is the suffering of change.

A very poor, underprivileged person might think that it would be wonderful to have an automobile or a television set, and should he acquire them, at the beginning he would feel happy and satisfied. Now, if such a happiness were permanent, since the person concerned had the car and the TV set, his happiness should remain forever. But it does not: it goes. After a few months, he wants another kind of car; if he has the money, he will buy another kind of television set. The old objects that earlier gave him so much satisfaction, now cause dissatisfaction in him. That is the nature of change; that is the problem of the suffering of change.

All-pervasive sufferings: Because it acts as the basis of the first two categories of suffering, the third is called, in Tibetan, *kyab pa du ched kyi dug ngel* (literally: the suffering of pervasive compounding). There may be those who, even in developed Western countries, want to be liberated from the second suffering, the suffering of change.

Bored with the defiled feelings of happiness, some seek the feeling of equanimity. This may lead to rebirth in, of the three realms, the upper realm that has only the feeling of equanimity.

Now, desiring a liberation from the first two categories of suffering is not the principal motivation for seeking liberation (from cyclic existence); the Buddha taught that the root of the three sufferings is the third: all-pervasive suffering. Some people commit suicide. They seem to think that suffering exists because of the human life, and that by cutting it off, there will be nothing. This third, all-pervasive suffering is under the control of karma and the disturbing mind. We can see that this is under the control of the karma and the disturbing mind of the previous lives: anger and attachment arise because we have these present aggregates. The aggregate of compounding phenomena helps us to generate karma and the disturbing minds; this is called *ne ngen len* (literally: taking a bad place). Because this resultant form is related to taking the bad place of disturbing minds and is under their control, it creates disturbing minds and keeps us from virtue. All our suffering can be traced back to these aggregates of attachment and clinging.

When you realize that your aggregates are the

cause of all your sufferings, you might perhaps think that suicide is the way out. Well, if there were no continuity of mind, no future life, all right—if you had the courage, you could finish yourself off. But, according to the Buddhist viewpoint, that's not the case; your consciousness will continue. Even if you take your life, this life, you will have to take another body that again will be the basis of suffering. If you really want to get rid of your sufferings, all the difficulties you experience in your life, you will have to get rid of the fundamental cause that gives rise to the aggregates that are the basis of all suffering. Killing yourself is not going to solve your problems.

※

We must now investigate the cause of suffering: is there a cause or not? If there is, what kind of a cause is it? Is it a natural cause, which cannot be eliminated, or a cause that depends on its own cause and therefore can be? If it is a cause that can be overcome, is it possible for us to overcome it? Thus, we come to the Second Noble Truth: the truth of the cause of suffering.

Strictly speaking, Buddhists maintain that there is no external creator. According to Buddhists, a buddha is the highest being, but even a buddha does not have the power to create new life. So, what is the cause of suffering?

Generally, the ultimate cause is the mind that is influenced by thoughts such as anger, attachment, jealousy. However, there is no possibility to cut the mind, the stream of consciousness itself. Furthermore, there is nothing intrinsically wrong with the deepest level of mind; it is simply influenced by bad thoughts. The question arises whether or not we can fight and control anger, attachment, and other disturbing negative minds. If we can eradicate these, we shall be left with a pure mind that is free from the causes of suffering.

This brings us to the disturbing negative minds, the delusions. There are many different ways of discussing the mind, but, in general, the mind is merely clarity and awareness. When we speak of disturbing attitudes such as anger and attachment, we have to see how they are able to affect and pollute the mind; what, in fact, is their nature. This, then, is the discussion of the cause of suffering.

If we ask, "How do attachment and anger arise?" the answer is that they are assisted by our grasping at things, considering them to be true and inherently real. When, for instance, we are angry with something, we feel that the object is out there, solid, true, and tangible, and that we are likewise, something solid and findable. Before we get angry, the object appears ordinary, but when our mind is affected by anger, the object looks ugly, completely repulsive, nauseating. Something we want to get rid of immediately—it appears *really* to exist in that way: solid, independent, and very unattractive. This appearance fuels our anger. Yet when we see the same object the next day, when our anger has subsided, it seems more beautiful than it did the day before; it is the same object but it doesn't seem as bad. This shows how anger and attachment are influenced by our grasping at things as being true and unimputed.

Thus, the texts on the Middle Way (Madhyamika) philosophy state that the root of all disturbing negative minds is the grasping at true existence; that this assists them and brings them about; that the closed-minded ignorance that grasps at things as being inherently real is the basic source of all our suffering. By grasping at true existence, we develop various kinds of disturbing negative minds and create a great deal of negative karma.

In the *Madhyamakavatara* (Entering the Middle Way), by the great Indian pandit Chandrakirti, it is written that first there's attachment to the self, then grasping at things and becoming attached to them as "mine." At first, there is a solid, independent "I" that is very big—bigger than anything else; this forms the basis. From the independent "I" gradually comes "This is mine, this is mine, this is mine." Then comes "We, we, we." Because of our taking sides, comes "Others, our enemies."

Toward I or mine, arises attachment; toward him, her, and them, we feel distant and competitive feelings like anger and jealousy arise. Thus, ultimately, the problem is this feeling of "I"—not the mere I, but the "I" with which we become obsessed. This gives rise to anger and irritation along with harsh words and the physical expressions of aversion and hatred. All these actions (of mind, speech, and body) accumulate bad karma. Killing, cheating, and similar negative actions result from such a motivation. So you see, the first stage is solely mental, the disturbing negative minds; in the second stage, these negative minds express themselves in actions, karma. Immediately, the atmosphere is disturbed.

With anger, for example, the atmosphere becomes tense and people feel uneasy. If someone gets furious, gentle people try to avoid him. Thus he, too, gets disturbed. And later, the person who got angry feels embarrassed and ashamed for having said all sorts of absurd things, whatever came into his mouth. When you get angry, there's no room for logic or reason: you literally become mad. So later, when your mind has become normal again, you feel ashamed. There are no good points about anger and attachment; nothing positive results from them. They may be difficult to control, but everybody can realize that there is nothing good about them. This is the Second Noble Truth.

✦

Now the question arises whether or not these kinds of negative mind can be eliminated.

The root of all disturbing negative minds is our grasping at things as truly existent. Thus, we have to find out whether this grasping mind is correct or is distorted and is seeing things incorrectly. We can do this by investigating how the things it perceives actually exist. However, since this mind is incapable of seeing whether or not it apprehends objects correctly, we have to rely on another kind of mind. If, upon investigation, we discover many other valid ways of looking at things and these contradict or negate the way that the mind which grasps at true existence perceives its objects, we can say that this mind does not see reality.

Thus, we must try to determine whether the mind that grasps at things as truly findable is correct or not. If it is correct, the analyzing mind should ultimately be able to find the grasped-at things. The great classics of the Cittamatra, especially the Madhyamika schools, contain many lines of reasoning for carrying out such investigation. Following these, when you try to find out whether the mind that grasps at things as inherently findable is correct or not, you find that it is not correct, that it is distorted—you cannot find the objects at which it grasps. Since this mind is deceived by its object, it has to be eliminated.

Through investigation, we find no valid support for the grasping mind but we do find the support of logical reasoning for the mind that realizes that the grasping mind is invalid. In battle, the mind supported by logic will always be victorious over the mind that is not. The understanding that there is no such thing as truly findable existence constitutes the deep clear nature of mind; the mind that grasps at things as truly findable is superficial and fleeting.

When we eliminate the disturbing negative minds, the cause of all suffering, we eliminate the sufferings as well. This is liberation or the cessation of suffering: the Third Noble Truth. Since it is possible to achieve this, we must now look at the method. This brings us to the Fourth Noble Truth.

∴✦∴

When we speak of paths common to the three vehicles of Buddhism—Shravakayana, Pratyeka-buddha-yana, and Mahayana—we refer to the thirty-seven factors that bring enlightenment. When we speak specifically of the paths of the bodhisattvas' vehicle (Mahayana), we refer to the ten levels and the six transcendent perfections.

The practice of the Hinayana path is found most commonly in Thailand, Burma, and Sri Lanka. Here, the practitioners are motivated by the desire to achieve liberation from their own suffering. Concerned for themselves alone, they practice the thirty-seven factors of enlightenment, which are divided into seven categories: the four close placements of mindfulness, the four miraculous powers, and the four pure abandonments (which are related to the path of accumulation); the five powers and the five forces (the path of application); the seven factors of enlightenment (the path of seeing); and the Eightfold Path (the path of meditation). Thereby, they are able to manifest a cessation of the disturbing negative minds alone, attaining nirvana and individual liberation. This is the path and the result of the Hinayana.

Among those who follow the Mahayana path,

the concern is not merely for their own liberation but for the enlightenment of all sentient beings. With this motivation of bodhicitta—their hearts set on attaining enlightenment as the best means of helping others—they practice the six transcendent perfections and gradually progress through the ten bodhisattva levels until they have overcome both types of obscurations and attained the supreme enlightenment of Buddhahood. This is the path and the result of the Mahayana.

The essence of the practice of the six transcendent perfections is the unification of method and wisdom so that the two enlightened bodies—rupakaya and dharmakaya—can be attained. Since they can be attained only simultaneously, their causes too must be cultivated simultaneously. Thus, together we must build up a store of merit, as the cause of the rupakaya, the body of form, and a store of deep awareness or insight as the cause of the dharmakaya, the body of wisdom. In the Paramitayana, we practice the method grasped by wisdom, and wisdom grasped by method, but in the Vajrayana, we practice method and wisdom as one in nature.

The Eight Verses of Thought Transformation by Langri Tangpa explains the Paramitayana practice of method and wisdom. The first seven verses deal with method—loving-kindness, bodhicitta—and the eighth deals with wisdom.

1. *Determined to accomplish all success, I shall always practice holding dear all sentient beings, who are more precious than wish-fulfilling gems.*

———

We and all other beings want to be happy and free from suffering. In this, we are all equal. However, each of us is only one while other beings are infinite in number. Now, there are two attitudes to consider: that of selfishly cherishing ourselves and that of cherishing others. The self-cherishing attitude makes us very uptight; we think we are extremely important, and our basic desire is to be happy and for things to go well for us. Yet we don't know how to bring this about. In fact, acting out of self-cherishing can never make us happy.

Those who cherish others regard all beings as much more important than themselves and value helping others above all else. Acting in this way, incidentally, they become very happy. Even politicians, for example, who are genuinely concerned with helping or serving other people are mentioned in history with respect, while those who constantly exploit others go down adversely in history.

Leaving aside, for the moment, religion, the next life, and nirvana, even within this life, selfish people bring negative repercussions upon themselves by their self-centered actions. On the other hand, people like Mother Teresa, who devote their lives and their energy to selflessly serving the poor, the needy, and the helpless, are always remembered with respect for their noble work; others never have anything negative to say about them. This, then, is the result of cherishing others: whether you want it or not, even those who are not your relatives always like you, feel happy with you, have a warm feeling toward you.

If you are the sort of person who always speaks nicely in front of others but says nasty things about them behind their back, nobody will like you. Thus, even in this life, if we try to help others as much as we can, and have as few selfish thoughts as possible, we shall experience much happiness. Our life is not very long: one hundred years or so at the most. If throughout its duration, we try to be kind, warmhearted, and concerned about the welfare of others, and less selfish and angry, that will be wonderful, excellent; that is really the cause of happiness. If you are selfish and always put yourself first and others second, you will finish last. If mentally, you put yourself last and others first, you will come out ahead.

So don't worry about the next life or nirvana: these things will come gradually. If in this life, you remain a good, warmhearted, unselfish person, you will be a good citizen of the *world*. Whether you are a Buddhist, a Christian, or a communist is irrelevant; the important thing is that as long as you are a human being, you should be a good human being. That is the teaching of Buddhism; that is the message carried by all the world's religions. However, the teachings of Buddhism contain every method for eradicating selfishness and actualizing the attitude of cherishing others. Shantideva's *Bodhicharyavatara*, for example, is very helpful for this. I practice according to this book: it is extremely useful. Our mind is cunning and difficult to control, but if we make a constant effort, work tirelessly with logical reasoning and careful analysis, we shall be able to control it and change it for the better.

Some Western psychologists say that we should not repress our anger but express it—that we should practice anger! However, we must make a distinction between mental problems that should be expressed and those that should not. Sometimes you may be truly wronged, and it is right for you to express your grievance instead of letting it fester inside you. But you should not express it with anger. If you foster disturbing negative minds, such as anger, they will become a part of your personality: each time you express anger, it becomes easier to express it again. You do it more and more until you are simply a furious person completely out of control. Thus, in terms of our mental problems, there are certainly some that are properly expressed but others that are not. At first, when you try to control disturbing negative minds, it is difficult. The first day, the first week, the first month, you cannot control them well. But if you make a constant effort, gradually your negativities will decrease. A progress in the development of the mind does not come about by taking medicines or other chemical substances, it depends on controlling the mind.

Thus, if we want to fulfill our wishes, be they temporal or ultimate, we should rely on other sentient beings much more than on wish-granting gems, and cherish them above all else.

Is the whole purpose of this practice to improve our mind or to do something to help others? Which is more important?

Both are important. First, if we do not have pure motivation, whatever we do may not be satisfactory. Thus, the first thing we should do is to cultivate pure motivation. But we do not have to wait until that motivation is fully developed before actually doing something to help others. Of course, to help others in the most effective way possible, we have to be fully enlightened buddhas. Even to help others extensively, we need to have attained one of the levels of a bodhisattva, that is, to have had the experience of a direct, nonconceptual perception of the reality of voidness and to have achieved the powers of extrasensory perception. Nonetheless, there are many levels of help we can offer others. Even before we have achieved these qualities, we can try to act like bodhisattvas, though naturally our actions will be less effective than theirs.

Therefore, without waiting until we are fully qualified, we can generate a good motivation and, with that, try to help others as best we can. This, I think, is a more balanced approach, and better than simply staying somewhere in isolation, meditating and reciting. However, this depends very much on the individual. If someone is confident that by staying in a remote place he can gain a definite realization within a certain period, that is different. Perhaps it is best to spend half our time in active work and the other half in meditation.

Tibet was a Buddhist country. If these values which you are describing are Buddhist ones, why was there so much imbalance in Tibetan society?

Human weakness. Although Tibet was certainly a Buddhist country, it had its share of bad, corrupt people. Even some of the religious institutions, the monasteries, became corrupt and turned into centers of exploitation. But all the same, compared with other feudal societies, Tibet was much more peaceful and harmonious and had less problems than they had.

2. *Wherever I go and whomever I accompany, I shall practice seeing myself as the lowest of all and sincerely hold others dear and supreme.*

———

No matter who we are with, we often think, "I am stronger than him," "I am more beautiful than her," "I am more intelligent," "I am wealthier," "I am much better qualified" and so forth—we thus generate pride. This is not good. Instead, we should always remain humble. Even when we help others and are engaged in charity work, we should not regard ourselves haughtily as great protectors, benefiting the weak. This too is pride. Rather, we should engage in such activities humbly and think that we are offering our services to the people.

When we compare ourselves with animals, for instance, we might think, "I have a human body" or "I'm an ordained person" and feel much superior to them. From one point of view, we *can* say that we have human bodies and are practicing the Buddha's teachings and are thus much better than insects. But from another, we can say that insects are innocent and free from guile, whereas we often lie and misrepresent ourselves in devious ways in order to achieve our ends or better ourselves. From this point of view, we are much worse than insects, which go about their business without pretending to be anything. This is one method of training in humility.

3. *In all actions, I shall examine my mind, and the moment an unsubdued thought arises, endangering myself and others, I shall face and avert it.*

If we investigate our minds when we are selfish and preoccupied with ourselves to the exclusion of others, we find that disturbing negative minds are at the root of this behavior. Since they greatly disturb our minds, the moment we notice that we are coming under their influence we should use some antidote to them. We can counter all the disturbing negative minds by meditating on emptiness, but there are antidotes to specific ones that we, as beginners, can apply. Thus, for attachment, we meditate on ugliness; for anger, on love; for closed-minded ignorance, on dependent arising; for many disturbing thoughts, on the breath and energy winds.

What is dependent arising?

The twelve links of dependent arising, or interdependent origination. They start from ignorance and go through to aging and death. On a more subtle level, you can use dependent arising for establishing that things are void of true existence.

Why should we meditate on ugliness to overcome attachment?

We develop attachment to things because we see them as attractive. Trying to view them as unattractive or ugly counteracts that. For example, we might develop attachment to another person's body, seeing his or her figure as something attractive. When you start to analyze this attachment, you find that it is based on viewing merely the skin. However, the nature of this body that appears beautiful to us is composed of flesh, blood, bones, and skin. Now let's analyze human skin: take your own, for example. If a piece of it comes off and you put it on your shelf for a few days, it becomes really ugly. This is the nature of skin. All parts of the body are the same. There is no beauty in a piece of human flesh; when you see blood, you might feel afraid, not attached. Even a beautiful face: if it gets scratched, there is nothing nice about it; wash off the paint—there is nothing left! Ugliness is the nature of the physical body. Human bones and the skeleton are also repulsive. A skull and crossbones has a negative connotation.

So when you feel an attachment or love toward someone (we are using this word in the negative sense of desirous attachment), you should think more of the object's ugly side; analyze its nature— the person or thing—from that point of view. Even if this does not curb your attachment completely, it will help subdue it a little. This is the purpose of meditating on, or building up the habit of, looking at the ugly aspect of things.

The other kind of love, or kindness, is not based on the reasoning that "such and such a person is beautiful, therefore I shall show respect and kindness." The basis for pure love is "This is a living being. It wants happiness; it does not want suffering; it has the right to be happy. Therefore, I should feel love and compassion toward it." This kind of love is entirely different from the first, which is based on ignorance and therefore unsound. The reasons for this loving-kindness are sound. With the love that is simply attachment, the slightest change in the object, such as a minor change of attitude, immediately causes you to change. This is because your emotion is based on something superficial. Take, for example, a new marriage. Often after a few weeks, months, or years the couple become enemies and end up getting divorced. They married because they were deeply in love—nobody marries with hatred—but after a short time, everything changed. Why? Because of the superficial basis for the relationship: a small change in one person caused a complete change of attitude in the other.

We should think, "The other person is a human being like me. Certainly, I want happiness, therefore, he must want happiness too. As a sentient being, I have the right to happiness; for the same reason, he, too, has the right to happiness." This kind of sound reasoning gives rise to pure love and compassion. Then no matter how our view of that person changes—from good to bad to ugly—he is basically the same sentient being. Thus, since the main reason for showing loving-kindness is always there, our feelings toward the other are perfectly stable.

The antidote to anger is meditation on love because anger is a rough, coarse mind that needs to be softened with love.

When we enjoy the objects to which we are attached, we experience a certain pleasure but, as Nagarjuna has said, it is like having an itch and scratching it; it gives us some pleasure but we would be far better off if we did not have the itch in the first place. Similarly, when we get the things with which we are obsessed, we feel happy, but we'd be far better off if we were free from the attachment that causes us to become obsessed with things.

4. *Whenever I see a being of wicked nature, who is overwhelmed by nonvirtue and suffering, I shall hold*

him dear, as if I have discovered a precious treasure, difficult to find.

If we meet someone who is by nature cruel, rough, nasty, and unpleasant, our usual reaction is to avoid the person, and in such situations, our loving concern for others is liable to decrease. Instead of allowing our love for others to weaken by thinking what an evil person this is, we should see him or her as a special object of love and compassion and cherish that person as though we had come across a precious treasure, difficult to find.

5. *When out of jealousy, others treat me badly with abuse, insult, and the like, I shall practice accepting defeat and offering the victory to others.*

If someone insults, abuses, and criticizes us, saying that we are incompetent and don't know how to do anything, we are likely to get angry and contradict what the person has said. We should not react in this way. Instead, with humility and tolerance, we should accept what has been said.

Where it says that we should accept defeat and offer the victory to others, we have to differentiate between two kinds of situations. If, on the one hand, we are obsessed with our welfare and are selfishly motivated, we should accept defeat and offer victory to the other, even if our life is at stake. But if, on the other hand, the situation is such that the welfare of others is at stake, we have to work hard and fight for the rights of others and not accept the loss at all.

One of the forty-six secondary vows of a bodhisattva refers to a situation in which someone is doing something harmful and you have to use forceful methods or whatever else is necessary to stop that person's actions immediately. If you don't, you have transgressed that commitment. This precept and the fifth stanza, which says that one must accept defeat and give the victory to the other, may appear contradictory but they are not. The bodhisattva precept deals with a situation in which one's prime concern is the welfare of others: if someone is doing something extremely harmful and dangerous, it is wrong not to take strong measures to stop it if necessary. Nowadays, in competitive societies, strong defensive or similar actions are often required. The motivation for these should not be selfish concern, but feelings of kindness and compassion toward others. If we act out of such feelings to save others from creating negative karma, it is entirely correct.

It may sometimes be necessary to take strong action when we see something wrong, but whose judgment do we trust for such decisions? Can we rely on our perception of the world?

That's complicated. When you consider taking the loss upon yourself, you have to see whether giving the victory to others is going to benefit them ultimately or do so only temporarily. You have to consider the effect that taking the loss upon yourself will have on your ability to help others in the future. It is possible that by doing something harmful to others now, you create a great deal of merit that will enable you to do beneficial things for others in the long run: this is another factor you have to take into account.

As it says in the *Bodhicharyavatara,* you have to examine, both superficially and deeply, whether the benefits of doing a prohibited action outweigh the shortcomings. At times, when it is difficult to tell, you should check your motivation. In the *Sikshasamuccaya,* Shantideva says that the benefits of an action done with the bodhicitta motivation outweigh the negativities of doing it without such motivation. As it is sometimes very difficult, yet very important, to see the dividing line between what to do and what not to do, you should study the texts that explain such things. In lower texts, it will say that certain actions are prohibited, while in higher ones, it will say that those same actions are allowed. The more you know about all of this, the easier it will be to decide what to do in a particular situation.

6. *When someone I have benefited, and in whom I have great hopes, harms me immensely, I shall practice regarding him or her as my holy guru.*

———

Usually we expect a person whom we have helped a great deal to be very grateful, and if he reacts to us with ingratitude, we are likely to get angry. In such situations, we should not get angry but, instead, practice patience. Moreover, we should regard this person as a teacher testing our patience and therefore treat him with respect. This verse contains all the *Bodhicharyavatara* teachings on patience.

7. *In short, both directly and indirectly, I offer every benefit and happiness to all my mothers. Secretly, I shall practice taking upon myself all their harmful actions and sufferings.*

———

This refers to the practice of taking upon ourselves all the sufferings of others and giving them all our happiness, motivated by strong compassion and love. We want happiness and do not want suffering and can see that all other beings feel the same. We can see, too, that other beings are overwhelmed by suffering but do not know how to get rid of it. Thus, we should generate the intention of taking on all their sufferings and negative karmas and pray for them to pass on to ourselves immediately. Likewise, it is obvious that other beings are devoid of the happiness they seek and do not know how to find it. Thus, without any miserliness, we should offer to others all our happiness—our body, wealth, and merits—and pray for it to benefit them immediately.

Of course, it is unlikely that we shall be able to take on the sufferings of others and give them our happiness. When such transference between beings does occur, it is the result of some strong unbroken karmic connection from the past. However, this meditation is a powerful means of strengthening our mental courage and is, therefore, an extremely beneficial practice.

In the *Seven-Point Thought Transformation*, it says that we should alternate the practices of taking and giving and mount them on the breath. And

here, Langri Tangpa says these should be done secretly. As it is explained in the *Bodhicharyavatara*,
this practice does not suit the minds of the bodhisattvas who are beginners—it is something for
the select few practitioners. Therefore, it is called
secret.

In the eighth chapter of Bodhicharyavatara, *Shantideva says, "If for the sake of others, I cause harm to
myself, I shall acquire all that is magnificent." On the
other hand, Nagarjuna says that one should not mor-
tify the body. So in what way does Shantideva mean
one should harm oneself?*

This does not mean that you have to hit yourself
on the head or something like that. Shantideva is
saying that at times, when strong, self-cherishing
thoughts arise, you have to argue strongly with
yourself and use forceful means to subdue them:
in other words, you have to harm your self-
cherishing mind. You have to distinguish clearly
between the "I" that is completely obsessed with
its welfare and the "I" that is going to become enlightened: there is a big difference. And you have
to see this verse of the *Bodhicharyavatara* in the
context of verses that precede and follow. There
are many different ways the "I" is discussed: the

grasping at a true identity for the "I," the self-cherishing "I," the "I" that we join with in looking at things from the viewpoint of others, and so forth. You have to see the discussion of the self in these different contexts.

If it really benefits others, if it benefits even one sentient being, it is appropriate for us to take upon ourselves the sufferings of the three realms of existence or to go to one of the hells, and we should have the courage to do this. In order to reach enlightenment for the sake of sentient beings, we should be happy and willing to spend countless eons in the lowest hell, Avici. This is what taking upon ourselves the harm that afflicts others refers to.

What would we have to do to get to the lowest hell?

One has to develop the courage to be willing to go to one of the hells; it doesn't mean you actually have to go there. When the Kadampa geshe, Chekawa, was dying, he suddenly called his disciples and asked them to make special offerings, ceremonies, and prayers for him because his practice had been unsuccessful. The disciples were upset because they thought something terrible was about to happen. However, the geshe explained that although all his life he had been praying to be born in the various hells for the benefit of others, he was now receiving a pure vision of what was to follow—he was going to be reborn in a pure land instead of the hells. In the same way, if we develop a strong, sincere wish to be reborn in the lower realms for the benefit of others, we accumulate a vast amount of merit that brings about the opposite result.

That's why I always say, if we are going to be selfish, we should be wisely selfish. Real, or narrow, selfishness causes us to go down; wise selfishness brings us Buddhahood. That's really wise! Unfortunately, what we usually do is to get attached to Buddhahood. From the scriptures we understand that to attain Buddhahood, we need bodhicitta and that without it, we can't become enlightened; thus we think, "I want Buddhahood; therefore, I have to practice bodhicitta." We are not so concerned about bodhicitta as about Buddhahood. This is absolutely wrong. We should do the opposite: forget the selfish motivation and think how to really help others. If we go to hell, we can help neither others nor ourselves. How can we help? Not just by giving them something or performing miracles, but by teaching dharma. However, first we must be qualified to teach.

At present, we cannot explain the whole path:

all the practices and experiences that one person has to go through from the first stage up to the last, enlightenment. Perhaps we can explain some of the early stages through our experience, but not much more than that. To be able to help others by leading them along the entire path to enlightenment, we must first enlighten ourselves. For this reason, we should practice bodhicitta. This is different from our usual way of thinking, where we are *compelled* to think of others and dedicate our heart to them because of a selfish concern for our enlightenment. This way of going about things is false, a sort of lie.

I read in a book that just by practicing dharma, we prevent nine generations of our relatives from rebirth in hell. Is this true?

This is a little bit of advertising! In fact, it is possible that something like this could happen, but in general, it is not so simple. Take, for example, our reciting *Om Mani Pedme Hung* and dedicating the merit of that to our attaining enlightenment rapidly for the benefit of all sentient beings. We cannot say that just by reciting mantras, we shall quickly attain enlightenment, but we can say that such practices act as contributory causes for enlightenment. Likewise, while our practicing dharma will not by itself protect our relatives from lower rebirths, it may act as a contributory cause for this. If this were not the case, if our practice could act as the principal cause of a result experienced by others, it would contradict the law of karma, the relationship between cause and effect. Then, we could simply sit back and relax and let all the buddhas and bodhisattvas do everything for us; we would not have to take any responsibility for our welfare.

However, the Fully Enlightened One said that all he can do is to teach us the dharma, the path to liberation from suffering; it is up to us to put it into practice—he washed his hands of that responsibility! Buddhism teaches us that there is no creator and that we create everything for ourselves; we therefore are our own masters—within the limits of the law of cause and effect. And this law of karma teaches us that if we do good, we shall experience good results; if we do bad things, we shall experience unhappiness.

How do we cultivate patience?

There are many methods. Knowledge of, and faith in, the law of karma engenders patience. You realize, "This suffering which I'm experiencing is entirely my own fault, the result of actions I created in the past. Since I can't escape it, I have to put up with it. However, if I want to avoid suffering in the future, I can do so by cultivating virtues such as patience. Getting irritated or angry with this suffering will only create negative karma, the cause for future misfortune." This is one way of practicing patience.

You can also meditate on the suffering nature of the body: "This body and mind are the basis for all kinds of suffering; it is natural and by no means unexpected that suffering should arise from them." This sort of realization is helpful for the development of patience. You can recall what it says in the *Bodhicharyavatara:*

> Why be unhappy about something
> If it can be remedied?
> And what is the use of being unhappy about
>   something
> If it cannot be remedied?

If there is a method or an opportunity for overcoming your suffering, you have no need to worry. If there is absolutely nothing you can do about it, worrying cannot help you at all. This is very simple yet very clear.

You can also contemplate on the disadvantages

of getting angry and the advantages of practicing patience. We are human beings—one of our better qualities is our ability to think and judge. If we lose patience and get angry, we lose our ability to make proper judgments and thereby lose one of the most powerful instruments we have for tackling problems: our wisdom. This is something that animals do not have. If we lose patience and get irritated, we are damaging this precious instrument. We should remember this: it is far better to have courage and determination and face suffering with patience.

How can we be humble yet at the same time be realistic about the good qualities that we possess?

You have to differentiate between confidence in your abilities and pride. You should have confidence in whatever good qualities and skills you have and use them courageously, but you shouldn't feel proud of them. Being humble doesn't mean feeling totally incompetent and helpless. Humility is cultivated as the opposite of pride, but we should use whatever good qualities we have to the full.

Ideally, one should have a great deal of courage and strength but not boast about them or make a big show of them. Then, in times of need, one should rise to the occasion and fight bravely for what is right. This is perfect. Someone who has none of these good qualities, but goes around boasting how great he is and in times of need completely shrinks back, is just the opposite. The first person is courageous but has no pride; the other is proud but has no courage.

8. *With all these (practices) undefiled by stains of the superstitions of the eight (worldly) dharmas, by perceiving all dharmas as illusory, I shall practice, without grasping, to release (all sentient beings) from bondage.*

———

This verse deals with wisdom. The preceding practices should not be stained by the superstitions of the eight worldly dharmas. These eight can be referred to as white, black, or mixed. This verse explains that the practices should be done without their being stained by the wrong conception of clinging to true existence—the superstition of the eight dharmas. How does one avoid staining one's practice in this way? By recognizing all existence as illusory and not clinging to true existence. Thus, one is liberated from the bondage of clinging.

To explain the meaning of "illusory" here: true

existence appears in the aspect of various objects, wherever they are manifest, but in fact there is no true existence there. True existence appears, but there is none—it is an illusion. Even though everything that exists appears as truly existent, it is devoid of true existence. To see that objects are empty of true existence—that even though true existence appears there is none, it is illusory—one should have a definite understanding of the meaning of emptiness: the emptiness of the manifest appearance. First one should be certain that all phenomena are empty of true existence. Then later, when that which has an absolute nature appears to be truly existent, one refutes the true existence by recalling one's previous ascertainment of the total absence of true existence. When one puts together these two—the appearance of true existence and its emptiness as previously experienced—one discovers the illusoriness of phenomena.

Now there is no need for a separate explanation of the way things appear as illusory from that which has just been given.

This text explains practices up to the meditation on mere emptiness. In tantric teachings, such as the Guhyasamaja Tantra, what is called illusory is completely separate; in this verse what is called illusory does not have to be shown separately. Thus, the true existence of that which has an absolute nature is the object of refutation and should be refuted. The illusory appearance of things arises indirectly: they seem to be truly existent but they are not.

How can something that is unfindable, and which exists merely by illusion, function?

That's very difficult. If you can realize that subject and action exist by reason of their being dependent arisings, emptiness will appear in dependent arising. This is the most difficult thing to understand.

If you have realized noninherent existence well, the experience of existent objects speaks for itself. That they exist by nature is refuted by logic, and you can be convinced by logic that things do not— there is no way that they can—inherently exist. Yet they definitely do exist because we experience them. So how do they exist? Merely by the power of name. This is not saying that they don't exist; it is never said that things do not exist. What is said is that they exist by the power of name. This is a difficult point; something that you can understand slowly through experience.

First you have to analyze whether things exist truly or not, actually findably or not—you can't find them. But if we say that they don't exist at all, this is a mistake, because we do experience them. We can't prove through logic that things exist findably, but we do know through our experience that they exist. Thus, we can make a definite conclusion that things do exist. Now, if things exist, there are two ways in which they can do so: either from their own base or by being under the control of other factors; that is, either completely independently or dependently. Since logic disproves that things exist independently, the only way they can exist is dependently.

Upon what do things depend for their existence? They depend upon the base that is labeled and the thought that labels. If they could be found when searched for, they should exist by their own nature, and thus the Madhyamika scriptures, which say that things do not exist by their own nature, would be wrong. However, you can't find things when you search for them. What you do find is something that exists under the control of other factors, that is therefore said to exist merely in name. The word "merely" here indicates that something is being cut off. This is not saying that there is no meaning to things other than their names, or that the meaning that is not the name is not the object of a valid mind. What it cuts off is that it exists by something other than the power of name. Things exist merely by the power of name, but they have meaning, and that meaning is the object of a valid mind. But the nature of things is such that they exist simply by the power of name.

There is no other alternative, only the force of name. That does not mean that besides the name, there is nothing. There is the thing, there is a meaning, there is a name. What is the meaning? The meaning also exists merely in name.

Are "mind" and "consciousness" equivalent terms?

There are distinctions made in Tibetan, but it is difficult to say whether the English words carry the same connotations. Where "mind" refers to primary consciousness, it would probably be the same as "consciousness." In Tibetan, "awareness" is the general term and is divided into primary consciousness and (secondary) mental factors, both of which are further subdivided. Also, when we speak of awareness, there are mental and sensory awareness, and the former has many subdivisions into various degrees of roughness and subtlety. It is difficult to say whether or not the English words correspond to the Tibetan ones in terms of precision.

Is the mind something that really exists or is it an illusion too?

It's the same thing. According to the Prasangika Madhyamika, the highest, most precise view, it is the same thing whether it is an external object or the internal consciousness that apprehends it. Both exist by the power of name; neither is truly existent. Thought exists merely in name; so do voidness, buddha, good, bad, and indifferent. Everything exists solely by the power of name.

When we say "name only," there is no way to understand what it means other than that it cuts off meanings that are not only name. If you take a real person and a phantom person, both are the same in that they exist merely by name, but there is a difference between them. Whatever exists or does not exist is merely labeled, but in name, some things exist and others do not.

According to the Mind-Only school, external phenomena appear to inherently exist but are in fact empty of external, inherent existence, whereas the mind is truly existent. I think this is enough about Buddhist tenets for now.

Index

Index

FOR THE BEST IN PAPERBACKS, LOOK FOR THE 🐧

In every corner of the world, on every subject under the sun, Penguin represents quality and variety—the very best in publishing today.

For complete information about books available from Penguin—including Penguin Classics, Penguin Compass, and Puffins—and how to order them, write to us at the appropriate address below. Please note that for copyright reasons the selection of books varies from country to country.

In the United States: Please write to *Penguin Group (USA), P.O. Box 12289 Dept. B, Newark, New Jersey 07101-5289* or call 1-800-788-6262.

In the United Kingdom: Please write to *Dept. EP, Penguin Books Ltd, Bath Road, Harmondsworth, West Drayton, Middlesex UB7 0DA.*

In Canada: Please write to *Penguin Books Canada Ltd, 90 Eglinton Avenue East, Suite 700, Toronto, Ontario M4P 2Y3.*

In Australia: Please write to *Penguin Books Australia Ltd, P.O. Box 257, Ringwood, Victoria 3134.*

In New Zealand: Please write to *Penguin Books (NZ) Ltd, Private Bag 102902, North Shore Mail Centre, Auckland 10.*

In India: Please write to *Penguin Books India Pvt Ltd, 11 Panchsheel Shopping Centre, Panchsheel Park, New Delhi 110 017.*

In the Netherlands: Please write to *Penguin Books Netherlands bv, Postbus 3507, NL-1001 AH Amsterdam.*

In Germany: Please write to *Penguin Books Deutschland GmbH, Metzlerstrasse 26, 60594 Frankfurt am Main.*

In Spain: Please write to *Penguin Books S. A., Bravo Murillo 19, 1° B, 28015 Madrid.*

In Italy: Please write to *Penguin Italia s.r.l., Via Benedetto Croce 2, 20094 Corsico, Milano.*

In France: Please write to *Penguin France, Le Carré Wilson, 62 rue Benjamin Baillaud, 31500 Toulouse.*

In Japan: Please write to *Penguin Books Japan Ltd, Kaneko Building, 2-3-25 Koraku, Bunkyo-Ku, Tokyo 112.*

In South Africa: Please write to *Penguin Books South Africa (Pty) Ltd, Private Bag X14, Parkview, 2122 Johannesburg.*